WHITBY
MODERN SEAPORT

by

Bernard McCall

MARY COAST, registered in Guernsey, is seen leaving the port in ballast for Grangemouth on 5 August 1986. In the upper left hand corner of the photograph can be seen the ruins of Whitby Abbey, and to the right, St. Mary's Parish Church. The photograph was taken from the top of the lighthouse on the West Pier.

INTRODUCTION

There can be few people who are not moved by the sight of a ship. Liners, with their promise of luxury and distant lands; warships, sleek and full of menace; tugs, effortlessly assisting giant tankers and containerships in narrow channels or harbour areas; and coasters, with a special fascination of their own. Coasters carry their cargoes to and from many small ports and yet they are often taken for granted, their vital work ignored. This book is intended to redress the balance by looking at the ships and trade of one small British port, Whitby, over a period of three decades.

I have approached the subject from an annalistic viewpoint, looking at how trading patterns have changed year by year. I have tried to highlight the development and decline of the most significant trades, while also picking out interesting occasional cargoes. Unusual ships are also given special mention in addition to those carrying the port's customary cargoes. As the book is aimed at the general reader rather than the enthusiast, I have decided not to give the gross tonnage and year of build of each ship as is generally done in books targeted at enthusiasts. It was felt, though, that the nationality of the vessels would be of interest so this is noted in the text, occasionally with the port of registry.

I wrote a short article, published in December 1979, for the magazine "Sea Breezes" on the subject of Whitby's trade between 1958 and 1978. It was the favourable reaction to that article which encouraged me to begin a more detailed study. I acknowledge the willingness of "Sea Breezes" to allow me to reproduce certain items first published there. I also wish to acknowledge the help given, directly or indirectly, by the "Whitby Gazette" - Whitby's weekly paper; Lloyd's Register of Shipping; and the two most recent Whitby harbourmasters, Capt. David Stevenson and Capt. Gordon Cook. My main debt of gratitude is to Mr. Roger A. Willison, of Whitby Port Services, whose interest in my research into Whitby port has never failed and who has provided me with access to his company's records and filled many gaps from his own knowledge. Any errors are entirely my own responsibility.

To Doreen, without whom this book would never have been written.

CHAPTER 1 1958 - 1964 :
LIMESTONE AND TIMBER

For some 30 years, Whitby's residents and visitors have witnessed a steady stream of coasters sailing to and from the quaysides in this delightful Yorkshire town. Whitby's associations with the sea go back centuries; it will always be linked with the adventures of Captain Cook and it has an important place in history of the fishing and shipbuilding industries. These stories, though, have often been told. The resident and visiting holidaymaker tends to remain in ignorance about the ships to be seen visiting the port in more recent times. The purpose of this book is to look in some detail at the wide variety of coasters which have visited Whitby, and at the cargoes they have carried.

The first arrival of the modern era was on 29 May 1955 when the Dutch coaster ANNIE berthed with a cargo of 320 tons of potatoes. A 14-man team was recruited from the dole to discharge the ship, which was the first of half a dozen such coasters diverted to Whitby from Hull because of a docks strike. These, however, did not signal the start of a regular trade.

It was on 11 July 1958 that the Dutch coaster NEDERLAND anchored off Whitby, berthing at 0130 the following day. Her cargo, 134 standards of timber from the Finnish port of Hamina, was discharged by 28 dockers in 46 working hours at a cost of £1 15s 7½d (£1.78) per standard. She left Whitby on 17 July. On 27 September another timber cargo from Hamina arrived on a further Dutch coaster, REGINA. She berthed at 0430 with 137 standards and only 39 working hours were needed to complete discharge. She left for Sunderland on 2 October.

In August 1958, however, there had begun the trade which was to form the basis of Whitby's trade for the next seven years. This was the export of ground limestone from Thornton-le-Dale quarries to ports in eastern Scotland. There were thirteen such cargoes taken during the last five months of 1958, all in vessels owned by the Hull shipowner J. R. Rix. The first cargo was taken to Perth by MAGRIX, which arrived at Whitby on 1 August. She returned on 16 August to load for Dundee. The next two shipments were also destined for Dundee but the ship was JONRIX. It will be noticed that vessels owned by Rix follow a clear naming pattern. Another member of the "family" arrived on 30 October - this was BOBRIX, loading 513 tons of limestone for Perth. She returned on 4 November to load 525 tons, this time for Fraserburgh. She was back at Whitby five days later to load 550 tons for Inverness. A fourth member of the Rix family appeared on 21 November, this being LESRIX which loaded 750 tons of limestone for Dundee and Perth. A new discharge port appeared for the final shipment of the year for JONRIX departed on 20 December with 728 tons for Aberdeen.

The trading pattern established in 1958 continued through the next year. The four Rix vessels in the limestone trade were joined in February by the Dutch VICTORY and in May by the Leith-registered ROSEMARKIE. The year saw 62 export cargoes of limestone, and two new destinations were added. On 7 March, JONRIX left with 720 tons for Kirkwall and on 13 October ROSEMARKIE took 560 tons to Methil. The year saw a handful of timber cargoes arrive, usually in Dutch-flag vessels. An exception was the Bremen-registered THULE which arrived on 8 July. Clearly the shore gangs were gaining experience in unloading the timber for they discharged the 132 standards at a rate of 3.88 standards per hour and at a cost of £1 8s 2½d (£1.41) per standard.

During 1960 there were some changes in the ships on the limestone run. Most notable is the complete absence of Rix coasters. The shipments in January and February were in W.N. Lindsay's ROSEMARKIE and ROSELYNE, both built in 1939, apart from one cargo taken by a Dutch coaster. The Dutch vessels tended to take smaller cargoes. On 15 March, for instance, DONATA left for Dundee with only 230 tons. A few days later, FEM, registered in Groningen, put in to Whitby for shelter while on passage from Middlesbrough to Antwerp. 27 March saw a new arrival for limestone - ELWICK BAY loaded 290 tons for her home port of Kirkwall. She now took all shipments destined for that port although she also took a small cargo of 170 tons to the Northumbrian port of Amble on 27 July. She had arrived in Whitby two days earlier with 150 tons of scrap and 12 cases of eggs from Lyness, on Orkney. This had been her fourth call with inward cargo in two months. On 26 May she brought 21 tons of potatoes from Kirkwall, a further 11 tons on 24 June, and 50 tons of scrap and 96 tons of seaweed on 15th July, again from Kirkwall. She was an interesting coaster, built in 1930, and having traded for J.R. Rix as NORRIX between 1936 and 1946.

The autumn of 1960 saw a lull in limestone shipments. After ROSEMARKIE left for Perth on 8 August, there were no further shipments until 7 October when Lindsay's KARRI took another cargo to Perth. The only vessel to arrive in September was ELWICK

A view of LESRIX passing the East Pier, inward bound to load a cargo of limestone. (Photo.: G. Spark collection).

After discharging her cargo of Kraftliner paper, the Finnish BORE VII makes her way cautiously past the swing bridge on her way out of the harbour. (Photo.: Capt. G. Cook collection).

BAY, which arrived on the 5th with 170 tons of scrap and 20 cases of eggs from Inganess. Surprisingly, she sailed light to Hartlepool the following day. The most frequent caller in 1960 had been ROSEMARKIE which took 52 limestone cargoes. The year had seen seven import cargoes of timber, three of them in the Delfzijl-registered ADVENT.

There were only four limestone shipments in the first two months of 1961, but the number leapt to thirteen in March. ROSEMARKIE was still the regular caller, supplemented occasionally by ROSELYNE, KARRI and the odd Dutch coaster. A new destination was added to the list when ELWICK BAY took 295 tons to Long Hope on 12 April, returning with potatoes five days later. On 28 April, she left for another new destination - Stromness. Timber imports were arriving at the rate of approximately one per month, and tended to be in West German ships. Typical was the arrival of the Hamburg-registered LEOPARD on 29 March with 137 standards from Naantali.

By 1962, KARRI and ROSELYNE were calling just as often as ROSEMARKIE to take out limestone. The latter broke new ground (or should it be sea?!) with the first shipment to Montrose on 12 February. An unusual arrival four days later was VECTIS ISLE, appropriately registered in Cowes, which sheltered in the port for three days while on passage from Goole to Blyth. Most of the coasters loading limestone arrived in ballast from other east coast ports. A surprising exception was the Dutch JUPITER which arrived from Mostyn in North Wales to load 710 tons for Dundee. On 22 March Whitby saw a new ship in a new trade, albeit a development of limestone exports. The Rochester-registered LADY SANDRA took 220 tons of bagged lime to Jersey. A similar shipment was taken by LADY SYLVIA on 24 July; she had called twice during May to load for Scotland. It was not until 11 July that the year's first timber cargo arrived, on the West German HERMANN HANS. The latter months of the year saw trading at a much reduced level, the only arrival in September being the West German HINRICH KOPPELMAN with 156.5 standards of timber from Hamina. The year ended with 61 shipments of limestone, mostly going to Perth, Dundee and Fraserburgh.

1963 opened with a new regular visitor on the limestone runs - the Dutch NOMADISCH took ten cargoes during the first three months of the year. A new flag also appeared in this trade when the Danish LONELIL left for Perth on 30 January. Once again it was well into the year before any timber imports arrived, the first being 150 standards from Hamina on HINRICH KOPPELMAN on 25 June. In August, a completely new trade appeared. On the 14th, the Groningen-registered TEXEL took 247 tons of strip steel to Brussels, followed by DEMOCRAAT on the 22nd. Dating from 1930, she too was registered in Groningen. Even older was HUNTER which took 280 tons on 5 September. She was built in 1926. A total of 62 limestone shipments were made in 1963, one more than in the previous year, but the tonnage involved was 1,330 tons less at 25,400 tons. It is interesting to reflect that 1959 also saw 62 shipments but a total tonnage of 33,398 tons.

1964 was a significant year for the port for several reasons, not least of which is a hint of changing patterns of trade. The first four months were notable in that there was no regular ship taking out limestone but rather a series of Dutch coasters on single voyage charters. The timber imports began earlier than in previous years - 145 standards arrived from Gefle on 19 April on board the West German RIGEL. The year saw a total of sixteen import cargoes of timber compared to seven during the previous year. By contrast, the limestone exports had fallen to 19,475 tons in 46 shipments, the last one of the year leaving in LADY SERENA on 30 October. Mention has already been made of the fact that most coasters to load limestone arrived in ballast from other east coast ports. Several of these ports no longer see coasters, for instance Bridlington, Stockton, Arbroath and the Cornish port of Hayle. Such are the changes which the observer of the coastal shipping scene should note.

CHAPTER 2 1965 - 1969 :
RAPID EXPANSION AT ENDEAVOUR WHARF

Perhaps the most significant development in 1964 was the building of Endeavour Wharf. Cargo handling operations prior to this had been carried out in the lower harbour. The construction of the limestone shed in the late 1950's had been met with opposition from environmentalists, and the dust from loading had also resulted in much adverse comment. Rather than lose the trade, it was decided to use a piece of reclaimed land in the upper harbour. In the event, some 2,000 square metres of land were reclaimed, and a wharf frontage of 120 metres was constructed, with road and rail connections. A depth alongside of 7 metres HWST and 2.3 metres LWST was available. The limestone shed was transferred to this site, and the completion of the wharf provided the necessary basis for a rapid expansion and diversification of trade.

This became clear in 1965 although the year began very quietly. The only arrival in January was the Aberdeen-registered HELMSDALE which came in at the end of the month to load 400 tons of limestone for Dundee. This had improved to ten movements in March - seven cargoes of limestone and three of timber. Prior to this, though, a most significant arrival on 17 February was the West German coaster PATRIA, to discharge 385 standards of timber from Gefle - almost twice as large as the previous biggest timber cargo. In the whole of 1965, there were 29 import cargoes of timber carried in larger vessels than could possibly have been accommodated prior to the development of Endeavour Wharf. These 29 cargoes averaged over 194 standards of timber, whereas the seven cargoes in 1963 had averaged only 145 standards.

Another important feature of 1965 was the commencement of the import of Kraftliner paper in rolls from Finland. The first arrival was on 15 March when the West German FRAUKE DANZ arrived with 668 tons of paper from Kotka. She was followed on 10 April by the Finnish LOKKI with 708 tons of paper, this time from Hamina. From May onwards, shipments were arriving at the rate of 2/3 per month, often in ships of the Bore Line.

By mid-year, the changing pattern of trade was becoming quite clear. July illustrated the trend when there was only one outward cargo of limestone, this being 615 tons to Perth in ROSEBURN, while there were seven inward timber cargoes. Of the 45 limestone shipments in 1965, only nine were made during the latter half of the year. In this trade, ROSEMARKIE reached a landmark on 23 April when she arrived to load her 100th cargo.

An interesting development in the timber trade took place when CATHARINA, registered in Kampen, arrived on 15 September. She discharged 59 standards of boxboard and 316 pallets of hardboard from Lisbon. She made two further voyages to Whitby. She arrived on 9 October with a further 59 standards of boxboard, the balance of her cargo having already been discharged at Great Yarmouth, and on 15 December with a full cargo of 120 standards of boxboard. Unusually for a ship having brought in timber, on her latter call CATHARINA loaded 550 tons of limestone for Dundee.

Towards the end of the year, there were three new cargoes handled. On 2 October, the Dutch coaster AIGLON sailed for Ostend with 200 tons of waste sisal. On 23 November, another Dutch coaster, CARMEN, departed with 550 tons of barley for Hamburg. Finally, the small Danish coaster STELLA RASK arrived on 14 December with 207 tons of refractory materials from Snaeke.

The advantages gained by the opening of Endeavour Wharf continued to be most apparent in the enormous increase in imported cargo. In 1965, 49 ships had brought in cargoes but this grew to 81 ships in 1966. By contrast, the 47 export cargoes fell to 36, with only 29 limestone shipments. In 1966, we find various new trades and ships; it is worth looking in greater detail at some of these.

January, for instance, saw a cargo of 260 tons of sugar beet pulp taken to Malmo by the Stade-registered ESTE, and a further shipment of waste sisal to Ostend on board the 1927-built Dutch coaster SIRIUS. The month's imports included two shipments of paper, one of timber and one of refractory materials. Imports of harboard and paper from Kotka were arriving in bigger and bigger ships. The Helsinki-registered SOTKA and TIIRA measured over 1,000 tons gross, and BORE X had a gross tonnage of 1,269. A new cargo appeared when, on 29 April, the Dutch JENJO arrived with 160 tons of molar bricks from Vilsund.

The summer months were very busy, July seeing eight imports of timber. ROSEMARKIE was still putting in occasional appearances, lifting a couple of limestone cargoes in that month. On 8 July, the Danish PETER SONNE took 615 tons of barley to Skive. Yet another new cargo arrived on 14 August when the recently - built West German ANNCHEN FELTER berthed with 1,214 tons of pig iron from Koverhar. The first day of October was notable. On the p.m. tide, another West German coaster, MEIKE, sailed with the first cargo of heavy steel scrap destined for Oslo. This vessel was built at Goole in 1939 and had traded until 1962 as GLADONIA under the British flag. On the a.m. tide, LADY SYLVIA had arrived with 1,476 tons of pig iron from Koverhar. She had two claims to significance, being the first Liberian ship to arrive in Whitby and, at 1,336 gross tons, the biggest so far. The Liberian flag, often termed a "flag of convenience", is regularly seen on large vessels but has never been common on coasters. Yet another new cargo appeared on 10 October when the Dutch TOROSAND arrived with 570 tons of granite chippings from Gudvangen. October was to witness yet another first for it was on 25 October that the first Russian vessel arrived. She was the Tallinn-registered KUIVASTU and she brought 414 standards of timber from Kemi.

There were two shipments of barley in November; one of 648 tons to Santander in the Dutch DRAKA, and one of 425 tons to Bremen. This latter cargo left on 5 November in the hold of a veteran West German coaster, HEDWIG PANNBACKER, built as long ago as 1917. The year closed with yet another new cargo - 359 tons of sheet steel from Hamburg which arrived on 14 December aboard the West German ALSTER II.

Quite clearly 1966 had seen Whitby start to flourish as a port. There was no longer a dependence on just two trades, but an increasing variety of cargoes was being handled, particularly on the import side. This trend continued in 1967 when the number of import cargoes almost doubled to 150.

As early as 8 January 1967, a new trade was noted when the Rotterdam-registered ALBERT V arrived with 501 tons of iron rods from Ghent. On 16 January, perhaps for the first time in recent years, there were four coasters in dock together. Two British ships were loading limestone : FERNDENE for Perth and ROSEMARKIE for Dundee, while two West German ships were discharging : ANNCHEN FELTER had paper and timber from Kotka, and KNOCK had timber from Gefle. A further arrival that day was another West German vessel, QUO VADIS, which brought 337 tons of aluminium from the Norwegian port of Husnes. She returned four days later with 218 tons of finished aluminium destined for Haavik.

Of particular note in February was the arrival of the first Greek flag vessel, AMALIA. She loaded 1,098 tons of barley for Almeria. On 3 February, a significant new trade began with the arrival of the Danish MOGENS GRAESBORG with chemicals from Hamburg. There were to be a further 16 arrivals in this trade during the year. Shipments of paper were starting to increase to three or four per month, with arrivals from Finland being supplemented by smaller quantities from the Norwegian port of Trondheim. The Norwegian ARASJO made her first call on 7 January, and by April she was calling twice per month. She was replaced on the route in August by another Norwegian coaster, RAMLO, which had been launched only four months earlier.

An unusual cargo was taken out by the small British coaster KIRSTEN on 30 March when she left with 52 tons of plastic pipes for the tiny Shetland harbour of Mid-Yell. New cargoes were still being handled - the Dutch CLOTHILDA M arrived on 27 August with 405 tons of fertiliser from Ijmuiden; and ships were still getting bigger -arriving with paper from Kotka on 5 September was the Finnish CANOPUS, the biggest so far at 1,716 tons gross. The next month saw further developments. On 23 October, the 1932-built Dutch coaster DONATA brought 73 tons of electrodes from Amsterdam, a further supply later arriving in the Groningen-registered JELL, along with 105 tons of salt.

Timber was beginning to arrive from other sources. On 21 October, the Danish ANNA FREM brought plywood from Hamburg while a similar cargo arrived aboard the Dutch coaster VISCOUNT. This vessel was owned by the famous Dutch coaster firm of Beck's. It will have been noted that Dutch coasters have been regular callers at Whitby, many of them being owned by their captains. It is sad that such vessels were virtually to disappear during the next two decades. The transfer of many cargoes to road transport and roll-on/roll-off ships, coupled with the development of increasingly specialised (and expensive) ships, has meant that tramping coasters are far less common. The coastal ship spotter can still see Beck's coasters, though, with their familiar grey hulls and blue funnels bearing the white letter B.

Among the 23 callers in November were two Russians discharging timber from Umba. Both registered in Archangel, they were NIKIEL and MONCHEGORSK. One wonders if they really needed their crew of 23. The final item of note for 1967 was the arrival on 3 November of the Jersey-registered GOREY with 497 tons of tinned fruit from Le Havre.

The first sailing of 1968 was the West German UTE FRESE which took 598 tons of barley to Hamburg. She had arrived on 30 December with sheet steel from Hamburg. Reference has already been made to vessels loading plastic pipes for the Shetlands. They were to be used for work associated with the developing North Sea oil industry. On 10 January, KIRSTEN sailed with 94 tons of plastic pipes for the Shetland harbour of Sullom Voe where a new terminal was being built to accommodate the large tankers which would export the crude oil.

February saw a somewhat surprising revival when the West German coaster ISMENE took four cargoes of limestone to Perth. Sheet steel was now arriving regularly from Hamburg, but a new cargo for the port this month was steel rods from Brussels. The first shipment of 669 tons was brought by the West German ANNA SIETAS on the 21st, followed five days later by 642 tons on her compatriot LUHE. Limestone exports on ISMENE continued in March, two destined for Perth and one for Dundee. On 10 March, the Norwegian STOKKEID took 803 tons of chalkstone to Mo-I-Rana.

April was a busy month with several shipments of board and paper from Scandinavia. The small Norwegian coaster REITAN was regularly bringing in cargoes from her home port of Trondheim. The only export cargo of the month was an interesting one. Sailing on 26th was the Belgian coaster ROODEBEEK, the first vessel of this nationality to visit Whitby, and her cargo was 537 tons of steel rails for Bonnières. May began with a further unusual cargo for, on the opening day of the month, the Brake-registered HANNE-S arrived from Rostock with flax waste. Cargoes of limestone were still leaving for Scotland. On 31 May, Beck's SWIFT took 331 tons to Perth, while FERNDENE took 310 tons to Kirkwall on 22 June. The month also saw two import shipments of wire rods from Lisbon and two of reinforcing bars, one from Gijon and one from Koping.

Trade during the summer months was dominated by imports of timber from Portugal and Scandinavia, and paper from the latter area. Of the other imports, the most unusual was 32 tons of refrigerator parts from Helsingborg which arrived on 23 July on board the Danish SATELITH. An unusual export on 24 August was 249 tons of paper destined for the Russian port of Riga on board the West German JANE. She took an identical shipment on 6 October and then 390 tons of paper to Ventspils, again in Russia, on 3 December. It is interesting to note that by 1968 most of the coasters visiting Whitby were flying the West German or Norwegian flags, in contrast to the scene ten years earlier when British and Dutch vessels were most in evidence.

Imports of paper from Trondheim continued to the end of the year, brought by RAMLO or REITAN, but still new cargoes were being handled. 503 tons of copper slag was shipped to Bergen on 15 October on board the Bergen-registered STEINVARG. Earlier in the

Typical of the large Russian ships which visited the port to discharge timber was the SHEMAKHA. At high water on 1 June 1972, she towers over Dock End basin.

In the 1970s, the Norwegian coaster ZENITA called regularly at Whitby to discharge general cargo from Norway. She is seen here at Endeavour Wharf, on 1 September 1971.

month, a large timber cargo comprising 313 standards was brought from Umba by the Russian EDUARDE WILDE. She set a new record for the size of crew - 26. The only variation in customary cargoes in November occurred on the last day of the month when the Dutch CAROLINE arrived from Lisbon. Imports of hardboard from Portugal had been arriving at the rate of one per month. She brought in 122 tons of hardboard, but what was unusual was the additional 152 tons of tomatoes which she discharged. Chemicals were now arriving regularly from Germany. A typical caller in mid-December was ROLF which had brought a consignment from her (?his) home port of Duisburg on the river Rhine. She sailed for Blyth on 18 December but was back in Whitby only two days later when she called to shelter while on passage from Blyth to Antwerp.

The early months of 1969 were dominated by imports of paper and board. The only other arrivals of note in January were two cargoes of fertiliser. The new Norwegian coaster KVARTEN brought the first on 20 January - 500 tons from Oxelosund; the second arrived three days later from Dunkerque on the Dutch BALTIC. The next three months saw trade continue at a good level, but with little of special note. Limestone was still being shipped to Scotland occasionally. The Dutch VERITAS took 446 tons to Perth on 1 February; IRENE reappeared to take 461 tons on 25 March, again to Perth; and FERNDENE took 314 tons to Kirkwall on 5 April. There were two further shipments to Perth at the end of May, the first by HELMSDALE on 28 May, and the second by VERITAS two days later. The first Polish ship to arrive at Whitby was SOLA, which berthed on 21 April with 200 standards of timber from Gdansk.

June proved to be an interesting month. On 2 June, the first aluminium cargo since October 1966 arrived; this was 720 tons brought from Mosjoen by the Oslo-registered BLANA. The British coaster FOXTONGATE, registered in Goole and owned by Hull Gates Ltd., arrived on 22 June with 218 standards of timber from Ronneby. It was very unusual indeed to find a British ship bringing timber to Whitby; in fact, it was becoming quite unusual to find a British ship at all in the port. FOXTONGATE was the first British vessel since FERNDENE on 4 April; the 46 ships arriving between the two were all foreign-flag. A new cargo to arrive on 29 June was 577 tons of esparto pulp from Susa, brought by the Dutch COLETTE.

Of interest in July was the arrival of the small Dutch coaster EEMSHORN, built in 1935, with 246 tons of whitening from the tiny Normandy port of St. Valery-sur-Somme. August was a busy month, with most of the trade being paper and timber. On 19 August, ROLF was back in port. She made the short trip from Scarborough in ballast and loaded sheet steel for Duisburg. She took a further consignment on 8 September, while another Duisburg-registered ship, CRAIL, took 251 tons to her home port on 3 October. In mid-September, EEMSHORN was back with more whitening from St. Valery-sur-Somme. It was a profitable trip for she loaded a back cargo of refractory bricks destined for Antwerp.

Autumn saw ELWICK BAY making a couple of trips to Whitby. She arrived on 2 October to load 218 tons of roofing tiles for Kirkwall. On 7 November, she departed for the same destination, this time with only 87 tons of roofing tiles but 5 tons of doors and 181 tons of limestone. November's only other export was 268 tons of sheet steel to Hamburg on 12 November by the Dutch REGINA. December brought nothing of particular note, although there were two cargoes of steel rails to Bonnières in mid-month. The first, 400 tons, left on 11 December on board the Hamburg-registered KLAUS BUCK; the second consisted of 368 tons and was taken by ILSE M, again West German but registered in Brake.

CHAPTER 3   1970 - 1976 :
THE BOOM YEARS

The new decade began with high optimism for the port. January 1970 saw three shipments of a new cargo - crepe paper from Gothenburg. The first arrived on 5 January on board the Danish coaster BALCO, launched only three months earlier in Rostock. The next two were on Oslo-registered vessels - JOLITA on 18 January and NINA on 25 January. A further new cargo was the export of steel sections to Bonn. The West German DINALU took 219 tons on 2 January, followed by 258 tons on the 1930-built JAN GERDES, also West German, on 24 January. February saw two shipments of steel rails to Bonnières, taken by ALK on the 18th and SCHLEI on the next day. It almost goes without saying that these two coasters flew the West German flag.

March proved to be a very good month. Imports included crepe paper from Gothenburg and Uddevella, paper and general cargo from Finland, refractory materials from Lysekil, and hardboard and boxboard from Aveiro. Possibly of more interest were the six exports of steel. There were two consignments of steel sections to Bonn, two of steel rails to Bonnières, one of steel wire to Duisburg and one of steel sheet to Aalborg. All were taken by West German vessels. It is worth noting here that the total exports for 1970 were 17,650 tons of cargo, a threefold increase on the 1969 figure. Steel exports accounted for over half of the total. Some of the steel was destined for Norway, for REITAN, still the regular ship on the run from Trondheim, was now taking outward cargo. On 18 March, for instance, she arrived from Trondheim with 330 tons of general cargo and 49 standards of timber, and sailed to Stavanger two days later with 193 tons of general cargo. A further Norwegian coaster was in port at the same time - PALLAS, discharging 133 tons of sugar presses.

Noteworthy in May was the first arrival of the Norwegian ZENITA. She would become a regular caller, but on her first visit from Trondheim she discharged 291 tons of general cargo, sailing the following day for Bergen with 110 tons of general. It is interesting to note a change in the balance on her next call on 28 May when she brought in 117 tons and took out 423 tons of general cargo. She usually included a call at Grangemouth on her journey.

A very unusual feature in July was the arrival of three vessels for non-trading purposes. On 2 July, the Jersey-registered SOREL arrived from Strood for repairs. She sailed at 09.45 on 10 July for the Thames, towed by Thomas Watson's GRAYBANK which had arrived from Hartlepool on the previous night's tide. By coincidence, another of Watson's coasters, LADY SHEENA, arrived from Blyth for repairs on 13 July. She sailed on the afternoon tide of 17 July but returned for 1.5 tons of bunker fuel on the following early morning tide. She eventually left for her home port of Rochester on 21 July.

August was a busy month. The Hamburg-registered THYRA BEHRENS took 214 tons of nylon to Rotterdam on the 4th. The next day, STELLA RASK arrived with 210 tons of refractory materials from Snaeke. This trade was now bringing monthly calls by STELLA RASK or her sistership HELLE RASK. The month saw three shipments of crepe paper from Gothenburg, the third of these arriving on 30 August on board LYS-POINT. This was the first call in Whitby by a vessel owned by the well-known Lys Line, a Norwegian company whose vessels are distinguished by their bright blue hulls. By far the most significant arrival during the month was that of the West German MARTHA FRIESECKE on 9 August with 696 tons of steel from Ijmuiden. The importance of this trade to the prosperity of Whitby's port has been enormous.

There were two export shipments in September, both consisting of general cargo for Haugesund and taken by ZENITA. Imports were of continuing interest, though. On the first day of the month, DORTHE TY, a Norwegian ship, arrived with 708 tons of steel reinforcing bars from Caen. On the following day, the Russian TAKHKUNA brought 464 standards of timber from the White Sea port of Umba, just inside the Arctic Circle. Such vessels tended to have a relatively long stay in port; she was no exception, eventually sailing for Murmansk on 11 September. There were four further steel shipments from Ijmuiden. On 4 September, HELIOS W arrived - she was the first Panamanian flag ship to come to Whitby. The next vessel was also of interest - the British flag ORIOLE, owned by the well-known General Steam Navigation Co. The other two consignments were in Groningen-registered coasters, WEGRO and APOLLO 1.

LADY SHEENA was back in port on 5 October, but still not to handle cargo. She called to land a sick crew member while on passage from Blyth to the small wharf at Snodland on the upper reaches of the river Medway. A familiar vessel was back in mid-month, for ELWICK BAY spent two days loading 120 tons of steel piling for Stromness. There were no steel imports from Ijmuiden

Built in 1936 and still giving valiant service is Whitby's dredger, appropriately named ESK. She is seen here returning to port after dishcarging her cargo of spoil at sea.

JEMRIX approaches the swing bridge to enter the upper harbour at the end of her voyage from Ijmuiden with a cargo of steel. The date is April 1975, only a few months after her sale and transfer from her previous Irish Sea service, and she still bore a blue hull rather than the traditional green of the Rix company.

during October but MARTHA FRIESECKE brought the next consignment on 4 November. Interestingly, two days later the Dutch coaster BRINDA took 1019 tons of steel casting to Ijmuiden. She would eventually become a regular caller with steel *from* Ijmuiden.

Steel cargoes were now a prominent feature of Whitby's trade but the Kraftliner paper from the Finnish port of Kotka, although not mentioned in recent pages, was still continuing to arrive in substantial quantities. The reason for its omission is that it was usually handled by the same vessels, these being ships of the Bore Line. For instance, BORE VII arrived on 3 November and BORE IV on 29 November. A further four cargoes from Kotka in December brought the year's total to 29. The next most significant trade was that in timber and general cargo from Trondheim which accounted for 23 arrivals, 14 of these by ZENITA.

For the last few years, January had seen new cargoes added to Whitby's trade. 1971 was to be no exception. In fact, the year opened in spectacular style with the New Year's Day arrival of the Dutch VALKENBURG with 600 tons of drilling equipment from Benghazi. In terms of exports there were four shipments of caravans to Rotterdam. The fourth of these resulted in the Blue Star Line funnel colours being seen in Whitby for the first time. This well-known company has gained fame because of its fleet of cargo liners, and it is often forgotten that it operated four coasters in the late 1960's and early 1970's. It was the Blue Star coaster CROUCH which took caravans on 28 January. There were two further shipments of caravans in February, both taken by ORTOLAN, a sistership of ORIOLE. For her first load, she had arrived in ballast from Goole where she was a regular visitor. She left Whitby on 3 February and returned four days later with a cargo of 201 tons of flax and 47 tons of goat's wool from Antwerp. Her second departure was on 10 February. The month's two cargoes from Trondheim came on the Stavanger-registered MOKSTEIN. On each occasion, she returned to her home port via Grangemouth.

On 4 March, ORTOLAN and ORIOLE passed each other off the entrance to Whitby. At 21.00, ORTOLAN was outward bound with more caravans for Rotterdam while ORIOLE was inward bound in ballast from Whitstable to load a similar cargo. ORTOLAN was back in port on 26 March but for a very different cargo - she loaded 252 tons of malt for Kirkwall. On the final day of March, the Dutch coaster JUTLAND arrived with 704 tons of granite sets from Leixoes. April saw two further cargoes of malt taken to Kirkwall, this time by the Aberdeen-registered HELMSDALE. She was to become a regular caller in this trade.

May began quietly. The first arrival was not until the 9th, but the wharves were busy after that. The arrival on that date was the Dutch EQUATOR with 620 tons of barley from Tilbury. The British NIMROD brought a rather smaller cargo two days later. In between, a small Norwegian vessel, CASINO, had brought a shipment of aluminium ingots from Mosjoen. The only other cargo of note during the month was a shipment of 984 tons of carbide from Heroya by the West German KISMET, arriving on the 16th.

Sheet steel from Ijmuiden had been accounting for two arrivals per month, but this total doubled in June. All vessels involved flew the Dutch flag. A further occasional arrival of sugar presses from Norway arrived on 19 June, comprising 86 tons brought by the Bergen-registered BRAVOUR. July saw a further four shipments of sheet steel from Ijmuiden. These cargoes could be unloaded easily within one working day. For example, Beck's VINCENT arrived at 09.15 on 9 July, and she was on her way back to load a further shipment at 17.30. Particularly noteworthy during July were five export cargoes of scrap destined for various parts of Europe: two went to Rotterdam, and one each to Piraeus, Cologne and Pasajes. British flag coasters owned by Tower Shipping put in an appearance on the Ijmuiden steel run at this time. TOWER VENTURE arrived on 25 July, the TOWER CONQUEST made two trips in August while TOWER HELEN made one in August and one in September. In fact, August saw six shipments of steel sheet and coils from Ijmuiden, while the West German SCHELDE brought in two shipments of steel arches from the Rhine port of Duisburg.

September and October were full of interest. There were two cargoes of malt to Kirkwall, the first in HELMSDALE and the second in the Dutch CORONA. Heading much further afield on 15 September was the Danish LISELOTTE LONBORG, bound for Thessalonika with 983 tons of scrap steel. An unusual import five days earlier had been 170 tons of graphite from Skaland on the Norwegian BRILAND. Imports during the last week of October are worthy of comment. On the 23rd, Beck's VISCOUNT brought 501 tons of pig iron from Rotterdam. There had been no imports of Scandinavian timber since the Russian HIIUMAA brought 448 standards from Leningrad on 8 June. Now, however, cargoes from Leningrad arrived on consecutive days, each brought by West German vessels. On the 26th, GRETCHEN VON ALLWORDEN brought 152 standards, and SVENJA brought 280 standards on the

Above:
On 26 July 1982, CAPECREST is seen discharging a cargo of soya beans at Eskside Wharf.

Below:
Having discharged her cargo of chipboard from Rotterdam, LADY ANITA makes her way out of port on the evening of 31 July 1984, bound for Harlingen.

next day. Finally, the last day of October saw a new ship bring in refractory materials from Annenaset. She was the FRIGGA BUUR.

During the last two months of the year, there was a further increase in steel imports from Ijmuiden. There were eight cargoes in November, and the first hint of a regular caller on this run, for the Groningen-registered BRINDA brought two of the consignments and she had put in two appearances in September. A further interesting caller on 28 November with 707 tons of steel was the British coaster JOAN C. This was the first of many voyages which she would make from Ijmuiden. The final noteworthy cargo of the year was a shipment of 197 tons of crepe paper from Lilla Edet by the Norwegian coaster JOBB.

The import of refractory materials during 1972 and 1973 was handled almost exclusively by FRIGGA BUUR and her sisterships NANNA BUUR, TINA BUUR and TORA BUUR. These coasters were quite small, with a gross tonnage of 149 and of only 90 net tonnes. The latter two vessels, although built in 1972, did not serve their Danish owner for very long. In 1974, TINA BUUR was sold to Saudi Arabian owners whose trading name, Diving Service - Khalifa Algosabi, suggested a new use. TORA BUUR, however, sank on 2 June 1973 while on passage from Antwerp to Copenhagen.

February 1972 was a busy month with 23 callers. Four of the six Ijmuiden steel shipments were by JOAN C. Two Russian sisterships, PALIDSKY and KIHELKONA, arrived during the month, but not to discharge timber. Each loaded about 930 tons of malt for their home port of Tallinn. In fact, trade with Russia was running at a high level at this particular time. A further shipment of malt, this time 1015 tons for Ventspils, was taken by the Russian ANGYALFOLD on 18 March while twelve days later the West German DOMAR took 370 tons of insulating paper to Tallinn. On the same day, another West German coaster came into Whitby. She was NIEDERSACHSEN and was bringing 579 tons of fertiliser from Nordenham. This was the second arrival of fertiliser in the month. CIMBRIA, again West German, had brought 394 tons from Nordenham on 9 March. A couple of days earlier, Watson's LADY SARITA had sailed after spending a week in port for repairs while on passage from Amble to Ipswich. Trade was now very brisk, and April saw 28 arrivals of which only three were for exports. Two of these were malt, one for Tallinn and one for Vejle. Among the imports were seven shipments of barley from Tilbury. Two of the vessels involved are noteworthy. On 14 April, 850 tons arrived on board JONRIX, familiar from the earlier days of the limestone trade, and the final shipment arrived on 30 April on Watson's LADY SABINA. What a change to see a Watson coaster actually handling cargo at Whitby! May, too, was busy and some new trades appeared. On the 10th, the Danish JENBO brought 496 tons of reinforcing bars from Gijon for discharge at Pickering's Wharf. This privately owned wharf, on the east bank of the river and upstream from Endeavour Wharf, was very rarely used. The next day, the West German JUV, dating from 1939, took 335 tons of steel plates to Dusseldorf. A couple of Dutch flag coasters, FIDUCIA II and PROVINCIA, brought firebricks from Rotterdam, while from the same port came 299 tons of maize aboard GASSELTE. Registered in Gasselternijveen, this coaster was four years older than JUV.

It is worthwhile pausing to comment again that some trades had been continuing profitably but unmentioned for a couple of years. This account has concentrated on new or unusual trades and ships of particular interest. The better-established trades produced little of specific note in terms of ships or tonnages but they should not be forgotten. The whitening from St. Valery-sur-Somme is typical. On 17 June, the London-registered IVY B arrived on her third consecutive call bringing the sixth shipment of this commodity during the year. There was a steady flow of chemicals from West Germany, usually Duisburg or Hamburg. Not surprisingly, West German coasters were generally to be found working this trade. On 2 June, for example, OTTO, registered in Haren-Ems, arrived with 317 tons of chemicals from Duisburg whither she returned three days later with 322 tons of steel plate. On 6 June, the Norwegian TEANO arrived with timber and 212 tons of general cargo from Trondheim, sailing on to discharge the balance of her cargo in Goole. She was to become Whitby's most frequent caller for she continues to serve the port sixteen years later. The month of June witnessed JOAN C make five trips from Ijmuiden, while on 19 June her "sister" ship PAMELA C made her third visit of the year.

Greek coasters are not often to be seen in North European ports, and so it was unusual to find AGIOS NIKOLAOS sailing for Thessalonika and her home port of Piraeus on 5 July, laden with 690 tons of steel plates. She had recently been sold by her West German owner, for whom she traded as ORION III, so it is possible that she was on her delivery voyage to the Mediterranean. The following month seems to have witnessed a similar occurrence for the Piraeus-registered THETIS arrived on 31 August to load 788 tons of scrap steel, again for Piraeus and Thessalonika. She too had just been transferred from West German to Greek ownership, being formerly called GISELA HAPPKE. With only eleven other callers during the month, her visit was welcome. The only other point of interest was the arrival of the Swedish GUNILLA for shelter while on passage to Scarborough with a cargo of timber. She was of interest because she was launched at Oskarshamn in 1940 but not completed until 1945.

September was a much busier month. Half of the 22 arrivals were accounted for by steel shipments from Ijmuiden. ZENITA reappeared on the service from Trondheim after being absent since mid-May. She continued to return to Norway via Grangemouth while TEANO, the other ship maintaining the link with Norway, went on to Goole. The month's only export was 221 tons of malt to Kirkwall in the London-registered WOPPER.

9 October was a very busy day. Of the five movements, four were on the afternoon tide. One of these, the Danish JENLIL, berthed at Pickering's Wharf to load 389 tons of steel plates for Copenhagen. A potential pilotage problem was eased by the fact that another of the incoming ships was JOAN C. She was now on her 40th voyage to Whitby and had rarely used a pilot since May. Of other interest in the month was the departure on the 19th of 345 tons of steel rails for Le Lègue on the British SEA RHINE. In fact, it was a vintage month for British coasters. Among the others was the 1938-built EDNA B on the 27th, with the month's shipment of whitening. ZENITA departed for Norway for the final time on 1 November; TEANO was to operate the Norwegian run more or less single-handed for the foreseeable future. On 4 November, the Aberdeen-registered SPRAY called at Whitby for engine repairs while on passage from Hartlepool to Amsterdam; she sailed the next day. JONRIX was back in Whitby on 11 December, this time with a cargo of steel from Brussels. A week prior to her arrival, there had been two shipments of steel bars from Hamburg, the first of 501 tons on BORSFLETH arrived on the 4th, and the second, of 810 tons, arrived the following day on EDITH HOLST, both being West German vessels. The year ended with a further shipment of steel scrap for piraeus and Thessalonika. The ship on this occasion, departing on 21 December, was LEFKATA, again recently sold to Greece by West German owners, and formerly named GOLFSTROM.

January 1973 saw nine steel shipments from Ijmuiden. These were supplemented by one from Brussels, in the British GENA F on 6 January, and one from Rotterdam two days later by the West German RITA DOLLING. The latter departed on the p.m. tide of 9 January and was one of five movements on that tide. The familiar

Watson colours were back in Whitby on 20 January when LADY SERENA arrived for shelter while on passage from Middlesbrough to Whitsable. She sailed the next day. February was a busy month, and it opened in unusual style when TOWER PRINCESS arrived from Goole on the 2nd to load a boat hull destined for Colchester. Five days later, the Greek ILSE took a cargo of 571 tons of steel to Piraeus. She was the latest in the series of former West German ships working a passage to the warmer climes of the Mediterranean. Her new Greek owner has shown little imagination in making the change of name - she was formerly ILSE FELDTMANN. The arrival of CAPRICORN on 11 February with 764 tons of steel coils from Brussels brought a new flag to Whitby, that of the Netherlands Antilles. JOAN C remained a regular caller on the Ijmuiden run, and was now joined by the West German LEVERN. The latter arrived on 26 February, making her sixth call of the month, but she had to stay in port because of mechanical problems until 6 March. She eventually left for Hamburg in tow of the tug MICHEL PETERSEN which had arrived from Bilbao. March witnessed three exports of steel - one to Antwerp, one to Elsfleth and the final one to Piraeus on 31 March. Again, the vessel was a former West German ship, previously named CONBALT but now called HALIMA. Unlike previous callers in this trade, though, she flew the Panamanian flag.

By April, LEVERN was fully recovered and once again was sharing the Ijmuiden trips with JOAN C. There were still occasional export cargoes of steel destined for the Rhine ports - on 2 June, the West German OEMBERG took 510 tons to Dusseldorf. Similarly, odd shipments of insulating paper were going to Tallinn. The West German JOHN BLUHM was a regular caller at Scarborough with timber from the Baltic. On 29 June, she made the short journey in ballast to Whitby to load 414 tons of insulating paper. July was a quiet month, with the fifteen ships not taking any exports. The imports included three consignments of steel pipes from Dordrecht, the vessels involved being identical West German coasters NOTOS ar 1 CHRISTINE and the British WILLMARY.

A significant absence from the August trading figures was cargo from Finland. This was now being increasingly shipped to Britain in roll-on/roll-off vessels which used purpose-built facilities at Hull and Harwich. Of interest among other imports was the arrival of 640m^3 of timber from Papenburg on 6 August aboard the West German HERMANN SUHR and 795 tons of clay from Bilbao on the Dutch IMKE on 11 August. Three Beck coasters visited the port in September. VEDETTE and KOSMOS took steel sections to

The Gibraltar-registered BEL-SOPHIE needs a push from the pilot cutter to help her to swing on to Eskside Wharf in April 1975.

One of the frequent callers with steel from Ijmuiden in the mid-1970s was PARKESGATE. She is seen leaving the port in ballast, bound for Ijmuiden, on 25 October 1976.

Rotterdam while GRUNO took the first of three consignments of chemicals to Antwerp. This left port on the 8th; the next day, FLORIDA, registered in Willemstad in the Netherlands Antilles, took the second shipment and the British QUIESCENCE took the third two days later. The most unusual of the imports was the arrival on the 8th of 124 tons of general cargo from Mannheim on EMILIA. The closing months of 1973 saw substantial quantities of steel coming into and leaving Whitby, often on board the same ship. On 26 October, for instance, the West German KRAUTSAND arrived with steel from the Thames and sailed to Duisburg with steel on the following day. A Rix ship was observed in port on 8 October when BOBRIX arrived with 910 tons of steel from Brussels. During 1973, there had been 101 shipments of steel from Ijmuiden. Of these, JOAN C had brought 33 and LEVERN 23. All 24 cargoes from Norway had been handled by TEANO. There were seventeen arrivals of cargo from Finland, a drop of ten on the previous year's total.

The new year began as the old one had ended - dominated by steel imports and exports. On the import side, there were twelve shipments from Ijmuiden of which four were handled by the British GENA F and three by the Hull-registered IRISHGATE. More of her shortly. JOAN C was conspicuous by her absence. Four shipments of steel came from Brussels, three of these being brought by the small Danish coaster TINE BACH. Meanwhile, there were four exports of steel to Rotterdam, two being taking TINE BACH. On the other hand, the Irish CELTIC TRADER brought two cargoes of steel from Rotterdam. A busy but confusing period! Amidst all this, the Panamanian DANI brought 321 tons of wire mesh from Beverwijk on 21 January. She had just left the Dutch flag under which she traded as DANIEL; a simple change of name. Earlier in the month, JOKAR brought crepe paper from Lilla Edet on 5 January. She was an example of a new class of Norwegian coaster, and she and her sisterships handled this cargo for the remainder of the year.

Among the nineteen vessels in February, there appeared some new ships on the regular trades. The West German coaster DUVENSTEDT was on the Ijmuiden steel run, while DITTE HOLMO, a small Danish coaster, began to bring in refractory materials, her first call being from Uddevalla on 10 February. Her compatriot TINE BACH brought two further shipments of steel from Brussels and loaded steel outwards, firstly for Hoboken and then for Rotterdam. March proved to be a typical month, with the only item of note being another different ship appearing with steel from

Ijmuiden; she was the West German FRIDEL. Most of the timber imports were now arriving from Trondheim on TEANO; what timber she did not bring arrived in packaged form from Namsos.

April's most notable caller was the Rotterdam-registered SURVEYOR. She berthed on 5 April with 943 tons of granite sets from Leixoes, and it was one week later when she sailed, laden with 1,100 tons of steel for Bilbao and Gijon. The year's first consignment of chemicals from Hamburg arrived on 2 May, brought by the Cypriot MIMI HELENE. Most Cypriot ships are registered in Limassol, in the Greek sector of the island, so it was very unusual to find that this coaster was registered in Famagusta, in the Turkish sector. TINE BACH brought yet another cargo of steel from Brussels during the month, and on the 24th it was pleasing to see a Rix vessel in this particular trade, namely TIMRIX. On the previous day, another British ship, TOWER JULIE, had berthed with 859 tons of steel from Antwerp.

June was a hectic month, with 27 ships visiting the port. Steel continued to predominate including fifteen arrivals from Ijmuiden. Watson's LADY SARITA arrived on the 7th, but it will come as no surprise to learn that she did not come to handle cargo; she required repairs to her steering gear while on passage from Blyth to the river Medway. Apart from a shipment of steel to Pasajes, July's only export was 340 tons of malt barley to Kirkwall, taken by HELMSDALE. She had arrived, rather unusually, from Lochboisdale on the Hebridean island of South Uist. Summer holidaymakers and local residents alike probably paid little attention to the green-hulled coaster in port on 30 July. They may have recalled seeing her many times before, and it was only those who paid much more careful attention who realised that it was not the familiar TEANO but her sistership THURSO making her first call at Whitby. She arrived from Steinkjer to unload 191 tons of general cargo and 141 standards of timber. Crepe paper from Lilla Edet was now arriving in Norwegian ships whose name was prefixed GULL_____. May and June had seen GULLHOLM; in July it was the turn of GULLFJORD, while August saw visits by GULLSUND and GULLFOSS.

It was particularly pleasing to see British coasters much in evidence during the last few months of 1974. In September, for instance, the two imports of steel from Dunkerque were brought by British-flag ships. The second was TIMRIX on the 20th; six days earlier, the vessel involved was the Guernsey-registered PORTELET. A further arrival on the 13th was WIGGS which arrived for engine repairs while on passage from Hartlepool. Her larger sistership WOPPER arrived on 23 November with steel billets from Ghent. Two days earlier, the London-registered PORTMARNOCK had brought a similar cargo. F.T. Everard's FORMALITY was another British arrival on 23 November, berthing for engine repairs and eventually sailing six days later to Sunderland. A further British coaster appeared on 30 November when PARKESGATE arrived with steel from Ijmuiden. She would become a regular caller. This patriotic glance at British vessels has taken us past our discussion of other callers in autumn. Of interest on 3 October was the arrival of the Danish LIMA, built in 1930, with 368 tons of fish meal from Skagen, while the West German ANNA H took 411 tons of steel rails to Bonnières on 25 October. November's two shipments of crepe paper arrived on GULLFYK. Steel from Belgium continued to arrive throughout December. On the first of the month, the Famagusta-registered ANGELIKI brought 617 tons of steel billets from Ghent. There were four shipments of steel from Brussels, all in British-flag ships.

The year's trade figures show 140 shipments of steel from Ijmuiden. The most regular callers in this trade were LEVERN with 15 visits, FRIDEL with 22, DUVENSTEDT with 26, but way out in front was IRISHGATE with 40. This coaster had been purpose-built to take containers across the Irish Sea from the Mersey port of Garston. However, she was proving ideal for the Ijmuiden run, and, late in the year, she was purchased by Rix and renamed JEMRIX. Her last four voyages of the year were under this name.

If January was going to set the scene for 1975, it was going to be a rather dull year. The only arrival worthy of comment was the return on the 10th of our old friend ZENITA with 115 standards of timber from Norway. Fortunately, February provided more of interest. Arriving on the 14th was the Dutch VOLENTE with 493 tons of fertiliser from Vlaardingen, near Rotterdam. Steel imports during the month came from Brake, Duisburg, Antwerp, Brussels and Rotterdam. There were still occasional shipments of insulating paper going to Russia, usually Tallinn or Riga. It was to the latter port that the Hamburg-registered INGMAR took 433 tons on 21 March. However, steel imports continued to dominate trade, although the arrival of the West German ELDOR with 309 tons of cobble plates from Dortmund on 3 March was unusual.

April's most notable feature was the shipment of three cargoes of barley to West Germany. Two of the coasters involved, JAN HAMM and ELBEMARSCHEN, were themselves West German; the third was the Dutch ANNA DRENT. Earlier in the year, Pickering's

Wharf had been sold to Scarborough Borough Council and was leased to the local shipbroking firm of T.E. Kettlewell. The wharf was renamed Eskside Wharf. On 10 April, the coaster BEL-SOPHIE moved from Endeavour Wharf to Eskside Wharf. Formerly called HASEWINT under the Dutch flag, she had been recently bought by the Belantra Shipping Company, an Anglo-Belgian concern, and was now flying the flag of Gibraltar. The change from foreign to British classification and registry resulted in her having to undergo stability tests and meet other requirements of the Department of Trade and Industry. She eventually sailed for Goole on 18 June, and worked regularly on a Brussels - Goole and Medway service. She suffered a small engine-room fire while berthed at Eskside Wharf, and was reported at Whitstable undergoing engine repairs in mid-August.

Shipping movements were about one third down on the previous year. This was largely accounted for by the loss of Finnish cargo, as has already been mentioned, to roll-on/roll-off vessels serving Hull and Harwich.. Proposals were now being made to develop Whitby's upper harbour and consideration was given to providing ro-ro facilities. The immediate intention was to provide the foundations for a ro-ro berth, and build the berth itself later if the need should arise. In the event, the ro-ro proposals were not pursued, and the upper harbour development went ahead without ro-ro provision.

May and June provided minimal interest. The Dutch ROENDIEP arrived with 1089 tons of granite sets from Leixoes on 12 May, while the London-registered WILLMARY berthed with 307 tons of maize from Rotterdam on 25 May. A new cargo arrived in the Dutch RAKET on 1 June - this was 301 tons of illipe meal from Zaandam. She returned with a similar cargo at the end of November. Coasters bringing steel from Ijmuiden were now finding occasional back cargoes. On 31 May, JEMRIX took 925 tons of steel sections to Antwerp, and PARKESGATE took 1,043 tons there a week later.

After a gap of several years, the Lindsay flag and funnel colours were seen in Whitby on 9 July when ROSELYNE arrived from Lerwick to effect engine repairs. She continued her voyage to Rotterdam two days later. The month saw five shipments of maize, the first two from Amsterdam and the next three from Rotterdam. The first one arrived in Everard's FIXITY on 1 July. Surprisingly, Everard coasters have never been regular visitors to Whitby. On 17 July, the Danish GEMALI took 427 tons of insulating paper to Ventspils and, on the same day, it was possible to see a coaster flying the Singapore flag in Whitby. The vessel was SEA MAAS and she was loading 553 tons of steel plate and pipes for Rotterdam.

August and September were much busier months. There were several new cargoes and vessel types to be seen. On 1 August, the Danish coaster LADY KAMILLA brought 602 tons of maize from Rotterdam. Three days later, the Yarmouth-registered A. KING 1 brought 297 tons of hardboard from Bremen. Berthing on 8 August was the small West German CELIA to load steel sections for Duisburg. That same day, HMS UPTON, a fishery protection vessel, sailed after taking on fuel. There were six exports of steel during August, three of which were steel bars destined for Antwerp and all taken by Polish ships. GOPLANA took the first on 19 August, and KRASNAL took the other two on 21 and 28 August. The first of a series of potato shipments was brought on 17 August by the Dutch ROERDOMP. She was followed by the British TOWER VENTURE and Dutch MARJAN within five days. The port of origin of these cargoes was Hansweert. Whitby was connected with two unusual ports on 24 August - a shipment of 189 tons of steel pipes arrived from Gelsenkirchen, on the river Ruhr, near Essen. The coaster used was the West German HEYE-P, whose port of registry was Ostrhauderfehn. What may have been the first East German ship to visit Whitby was ZINNOWITZ which arrived on 29 August from Gothenburg with general cargo and 168 standards of timber. It is worth commenting at this point that there had been no arrivals of cargo from Norway since 18 February.

It is surprising that there were only six steel shipments from Ijmuiden in September's high figure of 29 ship arrivals. These six were shared between JEMRIX and FRIDEL which now dominated the trade. There were eight further shipments of potatoes during the month; five were from Hansweert, and the reader will probably need a good atlas to locate the ports of origin of the other three -Brouwershaven, Zaltbommel and Breskens. Four Beck coasters called in September. ELECTRON brought 610 tons of rice pellets from Rotterdam, the source also of PROTON's 531 tons of maize. VICTRESS brought potatoes from Hansweert and took barley to Hamburg; KOSMOS also brought potatoes from Hansweert. October also saw 29 ship arrivals. Barley exports continued with shipments going to Zwijndrecht. Ghent, Rotterdam and Oldenburg, while a shipment of wheat went to Rouen. The p.m. tide of 25 October witnessed two Jersey-registered coasters, ROMARK and NIMROD, arrive with sorghum from Rotterdam. On the same day, Lys Line's LYSBRIS berthed with crepe paper from Lilla Edet. The month's final cereal cargo was 800 tons of maize brought from Bayonne by the West German BARBARA BREUER on the 28th.

The Whitby pilot cutter was involved in an odd incident on 31 October. The skipper of a Grimsby trawler radioed Whitby Coastguard to say that he was making for the port with a woman stowaway on board. The pilot cutter met the trawler about one mile off the harbour entrance and returned with the woman. She claimed that she had boarded the trawler to say farewell to a crew member and had inadvertently been taken out to sea. A likely story!

November opened with a suggestion that the regular trade with Norway might return for ZENITA arrived on 4 November with 130 standards of timber from Namsos. DITTE HOLMO continued to bring a consignment of refractory materials from Amal every couple of months. Less than usual was the arrival of the Danish GROLLEN with 355 tons of herring meal from Esbjerg on 19 November. Two days later, general cargo from Trondheim at last reappeared, brought by the Tromso-registered WESTERAAS. As is usual, trade slipped during December, with only sixteen arrivals. Mention must be made, though, of the fact that eight movements occurred on 4 December, seven of these on the afternoon tide. One of them was TOWER CONQUEST which sailed for Antwerp at 3 p.m. but was forced to return two and a half hours later with engine trouble. She eventually sailed on 6 December. The number of steel shipments from Ijmuiden during the year had fallen to 106, over half of them made by JEMRIX. There had also been seventeen consignments of crepe paper, ensuring steady rather than seasonal trade.

CHAPTER 4 1976 - 1979:
EXPANDING HORIZONS

1976 began with a fairly quiet month. The only two arrivals worthy of special comment were at the end of January when the Dutch coaster PRIMAS brought bulk clay from Rotterdam, followed by her compatriot EFFICACIA with rice pellets, again from Rotterdam. February proved to be much busier and began quite dramatically. There were five movements on Sunday, 1 February. One of the arrivals was the West German coaster COLLHUSEN, arriving in mid-afternoon with 585 tons of maize from Hamburg. As she approached the harbour entrance in rough seas, she failed to respond to her helm and collided with the east pier. She suffered damage to her bow and to her hull below the waterline near the engine-room. Although she was making water, it was at first thought that the ship's pumps could cope. By 7 p.m., however, it had become clear that the coaster was sinking. Firemen were called but they had difficulty in reaching the water because of the maize cargo. Fortunately, as the tide fell, the ship settled on the bottom. A team of dockers worked throughout the night to discharge 250 tons of maize and this enabled the firemen to pump out the water. It was touch-and-go but thankfully the combined efforts of dockers and firemen kept the ship afloat although her cargo was a commercial loss because of the water contamination. She sailed on the morning of 5 February, bound for the Tees for permanent repairs. However, she reported further engine-room flooding when three miles off Staithes. Whitby lifeboat was summoned, and a tug joined the lifeboat in accompanying her for the final stages of her journey as the water was being pumped out. Two other coasters brought further cargoes of maize during the month, both from Rotterdam and both happily without incident.

Still with cereals, HELMSDALE loaded 366 tons of malting barley for Kirkwall on 6 February. Trade with Norway was showing welcome signs of revival. The month saw three shipments of packaged timber, two of which came from Namsos as did two general cargoes. Steel still dominated trade, though. Included in this month's figures were four shipments of steel sections to Antwerp. The first was on 10 February by the West German HOHEWEG which had arrived three days earlier with 566 tons of steel reinforcing bars from Oslo.

By contrast, there were no exports in March. On the Ijmuiden run, JEMRIX was now joined by the same owner's KENRIX and the

In 1976, there was a brief revival in Whitby shipbuilding. One of the biggest vessels to be built was JUDAIRAH, a ramped ferry destined for use in the Middle East. She was photographed on the slipway of Phoenix Shipbuilders in October 1976.

The pilot cutter keeps pace with THURSO as she leaves Whitby on 17 August 1977. At this time, she bore the legend "Wilson Line" on her hull, and sported the green hull and black-topped red funnel of this famous Yorkshire shipping company although she was not in their ownership. She would discharge part of her cargo at Whitby and then sail on to Goole. Part of her timber cargo is just visible on deck.

Dutch BRINDA. Two arrivals are noteworthy. On 12 March, the Singapore-flag MYRIEL arrived with a large consignment of 1575 tons of fertiliser from Bourgas, in Bulgaria. Lloyd's Register of Shipping had the ship listed as a "vehicle carrier"; clearly, she was not using her vehicle capacity when conveying such a bulk cargo. The West German WESTWIND berthed on 19 March with 1,032 tons of steel scrap from Vlaardingen. The significant feature on this occasion is that the cargo was taken to Teesside by rail instead of road, the reason being that the consignee's scrap yard was rail-linked. It was hoped at the time that there would be further cargoes for onward distribution by rail, but this hope was not fulfilled.

A second cargo of steel scrap arrived on 4 April in the Cypriot ANGELO V. Two days prior to this, the Dutch ANTARES took 402 tons of steel bulb flats to Cadiz. Perhaps the most interesting item of the month was the departure on 24 April of the Danish MERCANDIAN EXPORTER which sailed for Flushing and thence Tripoli with prefabricated buildings. This contact with the Middle East was a new departure in the literal and metaphorical senses, and it was to prove important. On 12 May, a similar Danish ship, MERC JUTLANDIA, sailed for Benghazi via Felixstowe, with more packaged huts and magnesite bricks. In fact, May was a busy month with virtually all trades featuring. There were cereals in the form of maize from Rotterdam and wheat from Wemeldinge, Dinteloord and Dunkerque; fish meal came from Esbjerg; crepe paper (from Lilla Edet) and refractory materials (from Amal) were brought by LYSBRIS and DITTE HOLMO repectively; and the East German DENEB took insulating paper to Tallin.

An interesting departure on the morning tide of Saturday, 29 May, was VIC 32 which was bound for St. Katherine's Dock, London. This small vessel of a type often, but not correctly, termed "Clyde puffers", had been derelict for over three years and had been painstakingly restored to working order. This vessel currently offers holiday cruises in the Western Isles and Firth of Clyde.

At this period, Whitby Shipyard was enjoying a revival which proved to be tragically shortlived. It was currently building mooring barges to be used at the Shetland oil terminal being constructed at Sullom Voe. The port, too, was involved with cargoes related to the Shetland oil developments. On 7 June, for instance, the Singapore-registered UNION CRYSTAL left with 275 tons of steel pipes for Lerwick. The month's only other cargo of note was 701 tons of steel bulb flats taken to Hoboken on 4 June by London and Rochester's INSISTENCE.

By contrast, July was full of interest. There were three further shipments of steel castings for oil rig legs, two taken by the Danish DANIX and the other by the Panamanian SAMBRE. On 5 July, BRINDA made her seventh crossing of the year from Ijmuiden with a large cargo of 1,210 tons of steel. After discharging, she moved across to Eskside Wharf and loaded residential caravans for Zeebrugge, sailing on the 7th. She returned with steel five days later, then loaded a further 21 caravans for Zeebrugge. In mid-month, MERC JUTLANDIA was back in port to load 498 tons of general cargo for Trabzon. It was unusual to see a Dutch flag coaster, EMBLA, arriving on 12 July with timber and general cargo from Namsos. All previous vessels in this trade had been Norwegian.

The Irish flag is not often seen at Whitby, but the first day of August found the Dublin-registered ARKLOW BRIDGE arriving to load 567 tons of steel for Rotterdam. On the same day, the British GLENROSA berthed with 362 tons of wheat from Bonnières. She had a crew of only three. This was beaten on 16 August when the Panamanian CLAUDIA VII berthed with a crew of only two. This fine vessel dated from 1935, and she brought 344 tons of steel bars from Brake. Anchored off the port while awaiting the tide, some observers looking only at her hull colour believed that she was a London and Rochester coaster. For several years, the bright blue hulls of Lys Line ships had been a regular sight in port as they discharged crepe paper. On 18 August, however, LYS-POINT arrived with a new cargo - 409 tons of PVC granules from Porsgrunn. Sailing on the same day was another blue-hulled ship, the Dutch EXPANSA. She had loaded 264 tons of general cargo for the Turkish port of Samsun. Nine days earlier, MERC POLARIS, a Danish vessel, had loaded a similar cargo for Piraeus, calling at Felixstowe to load the balance of her cargo.

In September, there were clear signs of the rapid growth in trade with the Mediterranean and Middle East. During the month, four ships took out cargoes, and the tonnages lifted were bigger. On the 4th, the Dutch DANIEL took 633 tons of general cargo to Samsun; on the 8th, MERC CARIBIA took 935 tons to Syros; on the 18th, MERC JUTLANDIA took 827 tons to Hopa; and on 29th, the Dutch INGER SMITS took 513 tons to Samsun. There were two ''MERC'' ships on port on 7 September, for while MERC CARIBIA was loading for Syros at Endeavour Wharf, MERC TRADER was loading plastic for Brunsbuttel at Eskside Wharf. This high level of trade continued into October, with MERCANDAN taking 709 tons of cargo to Algiers and Piraeus on the 2nd; HELLE STEEN 550 tons to Samsun, via Zeebrugge, on the 9th; and HELENE CLIPPER 1,037 tons to Syros and Hopa on the 19th. All three ships were Danish. A sugar shortage in Britain resulted in two shipments of this commodity arriving in mid-month. Everard's CONFORMITY brought 796 tons from Antwerp and the Dutch AVENIR brought 497 tons from Rotterdam. The latter ship loaded 140 tons of baled hay for Werkendam. On 15 October, a new ship arrived with steel from Ijmuiden. She was the Groningen-registered PAULINA BRINKMAN and she berthed with the largest cargo to date - 1,516 tons.

Trade tailed off somewhat in November and December although there were four further sailings to the Mediterranean and Middle East. The only two other items of interest are the arrival on 5 December of the West German BACO with 100 tons of oil rig machinery from Flotta, and the arrival of the first French coaster on 17 December when the Dunkerque-registered MOR BIHAN berthed with 834 tons of barley from La Pallice. Undoubtedly the most significant event of the year had been the growth of Middle East trade, but one or two other points ought to be noted. Firstly, the number of vessels arriving from Ijmuiden was one third down on 1975, yet the tonnage carried fell by only 6,000 tons. This was because the ships were carrying bigger cargoes. Secondly, there was some revival in the packaged timber/general cargo trade from Norway, mostly handled by ROSELLE and WESTERAAS.

The end of the year had seen another significant maritime event in the port, not directly related to cargo handling. Mention has already been made of the revival in shipbuilding in Whitby, and on Saturday, 6 November, a ramped transport ferry, named JUDAIRAH, was launched into the river Esk. 36 metres long, she was the largest vessel to have been built in Whitby for over fifty years. She took six months to build and was destined for service in Abu Dhabi.

The first five vessels of 1977 were handling what had now become the port's customary cargoes. LYS BLINK was the first to arrive, on the 3rd, with crepe paper from Lilla Edet. On the following day, DITTE HOLMO berthed with refractory materials from Uddevalla, ROSELLE with timber from Norway, and FRIDEL from Ijmuiden with steel. On the 5th, the Dutch ARINA HOLWERDA arrived to load 929 tons of general cargo for Samsun. The month's other export to Samsun was taken by the Dutch EDDA on the 26th. The pale blue hull of Paal Wilson's MYRMO, registered in Bergen, brightened the harbour scene in mid-month as she discharged 573 tons of PVC from Heroya. February also saw two vessels load for

Samsun, MAUDE ISA and QUINTUS, both of which were Danish and registered in Copenhagen. The middle of the month proved to be very busy. QUINTUS sailed on the 14th; on the previous day, JEMRIX and KENRIX arrived from Ijmuiden (the latter discharging and sailing on the next tide), LYS SKY arrived from Lilla Edet and KINSO, another Paal Wilson ship, berthed with steel from Porsgrunn. DITTE HOLMO cleared for Skagen on the 15th after discharging her usual refractories, but was forced to return for engine repairs in the early hours of the following morning.

March witnessed an increase in traffic, mainly because of extra imports. There were, for instance, three shipments of potatoes from Santander, the vessels involved being the Dutch ROENDIEP, the West German REINBEK and the British CAPECREST. On 21 March, TEANO arrived with general cargo and 86m^3 of timber from Trondheim, sailing on to Goole the next day to discharge the remainder of her cargo. She had become a rare visitor, not having called at all in 1976, and she would make only very occasional calls during the rest of 1977. Her sistership THURSO would make rather more frequent calls. On 25 March, the West German KERSTIN EVA arrived with 512 tons of chemicals from Hamburg. She had brought such cargoes, from Hamburg or Bremen, occasionally during 1976 and early 1977. On this visit, she loaded steel for Rotterdam. The month's most interesting visitor was the Dutch tug ANTONIE JUNIOR which came on 6 March. She sailed four hours after her arrival, towing the ferry JUDAIRAH to Rotterdam.

More potatoes were imported from Spain in April; there were two shipments from Santander and two from Bilbao. There were also two cargoes of barley from Rotterdam. The first of these came in the Singapore flag UNION GEM, which then loaded railway axles for Rouen; the second was brought by London and Rochester's PERTINENCE. General cargoes were still going to the Turkish port of Samsun at the rate of one or two per month. An unusual export during the month was 257 tons of concrete blocks taken to Sullom Voe by the 1941-built TAIRLAW, a British coaster, on 26 April. May was a quiet month, the only export being 730 tons of steel to Aarhus and Koge on the East German INSEL REIMS. She sailed on the 6th, having arrived two days earlier from Scarborough. Among the imports were two shipments of PVC, the first from Heroya by the West German ESDORP and the second from Cagliari by the Dutch KLAZINA. The month closed with the arrival on the last day of the West German MALENTE conveying 623 tons of soda ash from Szczecin.

The exports to Turkey halted temporarily after the departure of the Danish HELLE FRANK for Samsun on 16 June. The month's only other export was 623 tons of cast iron scrap to Rotterdam in the Rochester-registered HOOPRIDE. A particularly odd feature of the trading pattern this month was the number of one-off imports. Four are used to illustrate the point, but there were others. The West German HEDE arrived on 8 June with potatoes from Larnaca; on the 14th, our old friend CLAUDIA VII returned with grain from Bremen; Paal Wilson's JUSTO arrived with 705 tons of chemicals from Nystad on the 19th; and the Danish BAJOS TRIGON brought 600 tons of clay from Bilbao on the 23rd. There were no exports at all in July, and only two import cargoes are worthy of mention. On the 4th, the Dutch AZOLLA arrived with 512 tons of grit from Utrecht, and the same day saw the arrival of the British HALCIENCE with maize pellets from Bremen. The month's most notable feature was the arrival at the end of the month of the British tug WATERLOO which called to tow a fishing boat to the Tyne.

The arrival of the West German ANGLIA on 9 August with 362 tons of ammonium chloride from Ludwigshafen was the one item of note in an otherwise dull August, at least in terms of shipping interest. The month's six shipments of steel from Ijmuiden all arrived in different ships : FRIDEL, PAULINA BRINKMAN, JEMRIX, KENRIX, PARKESGATE and BRINDA. Other ports sharing this steel trade from Ijmuiden have included Dagenham, Rochester and Poole. September's two export cargoes did not involve new commodities. On the 6th, the British ANDERS W took concrete blocks to Sullom Voe, and on the 15th, GUY CHIPPERFIELD, again British, took steel axles to Rouen. Norwegian general cargo was still coming in at a steady rate, with TEANO now arriving more regularly from Trondheim and sailing on to Goole, and ROSELLE arriving from Namsos with timber, silicon carbide and wire, and returning to Norway via Grangemouth. Memories of the COLLHUSEN incident were revived on the afternoon of 28 September when the Danish SIRI MARIA, inwards from Brake with a cargo of steel, struck the West Pier. On this occasion, the vessel's pumps were able to cope with the ingress of water and she sailed on 2 October following the completion of temporary repairs.

There was a slight increase in the number of ships arriving during October. Most of them were bringing steel from Duisburg, Brake, Hamburg and, of course, Ijmuiden. The Norwegian LYS-CON was seen in the port on three occasions during the month, each time discharging crepe paper from Lilla Edet. October's last day saw a very unusual arrival when the Danish MATHEA LUPE arrived from Middlesbrough for engine repairs. She was the first tanker to visit Whitby. She sailed on 4 November, bound for the Isle of Grain and thence the Persian Gulf. The remainder of November and December found no new cargoes or interesting vessels.

1978 began with trade following what was now becoming a familiar pattern. New Year's Day saw the arrival of LYS BRIS with crepe paper, and her sistership LYS BLINK arrived on the next day. The month's only export was 612 tons of bentonite clay to Sandnes on the 13th in the Norwegian NORPOINT. Until the previous year, she had traded for Lys Line as LYS-POINT. There were still occasional shipments of ammonium chloride from Ludwigshafen and other chemicals from Hamburg. The West German ANTON HELD arrived from Ludwigshafen on 2 and 28 January, while the Hamburg-registered GORCH FOCK brought her cargo from her home port on 26 February before loading 480 tons of steel plates for Rotterdam. On 12 March, the Norwegian CAP CARGO brought 877mm^3 of packaged timber from Namsos, and the more usual ROSELLE arrived on 29 March.

It was the end of April before any truly noteworthy arrivals came. On the 22nd, ANTON HELD berthed with 419 tons of firebricks from Mannheim, and the month closed with two consignments of fertiliser from Antwerp, the first on the West German SEA ODIN and the second on the British WILLMARY.

By May, more varied cargoes were being handled once again. For example, early in the month there were two export cargoes of fertiliser in bulk. WIKING, a West German vessel, took the first to Husum, followed by the Cypriot TRAMP which sailed to Rendsburg. In mid-month, a blue-hulled Holwerda ship was in port but not loading for the Middle East on this occasion; GRETINA HOLWERDA was loading steel rails for Le Lègue. DITTE HOLMO had continued to be a regular caller with refractory materials, but her arrival on 14 May from Esbjerg brought fish meal. On 29 May, the West German ANJOLA berthed with 999 tons of fertiliser from Duisburg.

Contrasting with recent months, June had much of interest in exports. A new trade appeared in the shape of portacabins to the Shetland Islands, all in West German ships. On the first day of the month, RUTH GRAEF took 24 units; then, on the 23rd, DANIELA took 21 units and 73 tons of cargo in containers. Five days later, BACO took 11 units. All vessels were bound for Sandwick, although DANIELA called also at Sullom Voe. Another export, again handled

On 16 August 1978, PEP SIRIUS makes her way out of the harbour, at the start of a long voyage to Jeddah with insulation material.

On 17 August 1978, ELEONORA makes a splendid sight as she approaches the harbour entrance, inward bound from Le Havre to load portacabins for Shetland.

by West German coasters, was bulk fertiliser to their homeland. SEESCHWALBE took 535 tons to Cuxhaven on 2 June, and ten days later HEIKE took 463 tons to Heiligenhafen. The only import of any interest was a familiar commodity, crepe paper, but the port of origin, Norrkoping, and the fact that the ship involved, OSENBERG, was West German, were both unusual in this particular trade. Also unusual was the departure of KENRIX on 29 June with a return cargo, 182 tons of machinery, for Ijmuiden.

July saw further shipments of portacabins to Shetland. Both were taken by the West German NORDFELD which cleared the port on the 7th and 14th. Her initial arrival had been from the Russian port of Ventspils, a long ballast voyage. The lengthiest stay in port for some years was credited to the Dutch ROELOF HOLWERDA which arrived on 8 July with 1,112 tons of boric acid from Bandirma. She sailed ten days later with 497 tons of general cargo for Samsun, calling at Dunkerque en route. This was to prove the start of a new series of shipments to the Middle East. While ROELOF HOLWERDA was in port, LYS-CON arrived with her customary cargo of crepe paper from Lilla Edet on 12 July and she left four days later, laden with 532 tons of clay for Sandnes. Finally for the month, MAGU sailed to her home port of Hamburg on the 28th with 525 tons of wire rod and coil.

Although the number of ships in August was one third down on the total for July, there was still much of interest. A further two shipments of portacabins left for Sandwick, the first on the 10th taken by CORVUS and the second eight days later taken by ELEONORA; both vessels were West German. There were also two export cargoes to Samsun. On the 8th, ELISABETH HOLWERDA took 612 tons of general cargo, followed on the 18th by ARINA HOLWERDA, laden with 378 tons. Two days earlier, the Danish PEP SIRIUS had sailed for Jeddah with 92 tons of insulation material. On the 27th, another Danish ship, SABINE, brought a cargo of PVC from Heroya, and sailed on 1 September with 20 portacabins for Sandwick. She berthed at the newly-reopened Eskside Wharf. This wharf had been closed for over a year while land was being reclaimed on the opposite bank as part of the upper harbour redevelopment scheme.

September found three Holwerda-owned ships in port towards the end of the month. On the 23rd, ELISABETH HOLWERDA departed with another cargo for Samsun, while HAICO HOLWERDA had arrived on that morning's tide to load steel sections for Antwerp. This vessel differed from others in the fleet in that she had roll-on/roll-off facilities and was of low air-draught for navigation on some of Europe's inland waterways. On the following day, EXPANSA arrived to load 704 tons of steel plates for Nigg Bay in north-east Scotland. She returned for a further consignment on the 30th. These plates would be used in the fabrication of oil rigs being constructed at the Nigg site on the northern shore of the Cromarty Firth. The previous day had seen the arrival of PARKESGATE on her tenth visit of the year, but not with steel from Ijmuiden on this occasion. Instead, her unusual cargo was 211 tons of excavators from Hamburg. Speaking of Ijmuiden ships, JEMRIX arrived on 6 September after a four month absence. In fact, she called only four times during the year - the most regular caller was PARKESGATE, with 14 visits, followed closely by FRIDEL with 13. It should also be noted that there were only 46 arrivals in total from Ijmuiden; there had been 65 in 1977 and 90 in 1976. The final quarter of 1978 was a very quiet period in the port, with only seventeen vessels calling in October, ten in November and eight in December. Each month saw one export cargo to Samsun, October's being taken unusually by the Singapore-registered PERNA.

The new year began with scarcely more activity than the old one had ended, although 2 January did provide a little interest when ELISABETH HOLWERDA arrived with boric acid from Bandirma and LYS BRIS arrived to load 396 tons of plastic powder for Koge. February was much more interesting. On the 10th, a new type of vessel for the port arrived in the shape of the oil-rig supply ship SCOTOIL II, registered in Leith, which berthed at 2 p.m. to load machinery for the Stratford-A platform in the North Sea; her stay in port lasted only an hour and a half. Eight days later, an important new trade appeared with the arrival of the Hamburg-registered KISMET. She had come, via Middlesbrough, from her home port with 345 tons of general cargo from China. This cargo had been trans-shipped from a large freighter in Hamburg. On 26 February, the West German HEIKE arrived with 611 tons of silica bricks from Rotterdam; a further, smaller cargo of these bricks was brought on 14 March from the Rhine port of Andernach by the West German MICHAEL C which returned only ten days later but with fertiliser from Antwerp. Busy tides had become a thing of the past until 30 March, when there were six movements on the late afternoon tide, four departures and two arrivals. There were four consignments of Chinese general cargo during the month. The first two, on the 5th and 7th were brought by TORGELOW and RECHLIN respectively, both East German. It was soon noticeable that many of the ships in this trade flew the flags of Communist bloc contries.

On 3 April, a different, and rather ugly, outline appeared in port when the Norwegian COASTER CONNY berthed with 331 tons of PVC from Kristiansand. Her bulky forward mast/derrick, although no doubt very functional, gave her an ungainly appearance. An astonishing arrival on 18 April was the Danish SVENDBORG BAY which had brought 386 tons of general cargo, mainly honey and orange juice, all the way from Buenos Aires. Sailing on the same day was a vessel which did not handle cargo but it is certainly worth a mention. She was VIC 56, a wartime-built Victual Inshore Craft similar to VIC 32 previously mentioned. She had, like VIC 32, been bought by an enthusiast and was on passage from Rosyth to the Thames. May was a busy month with 25 vessels calling compared to 14 in April. There were three exports. On the 3rd, HELMSDALE took 344 tons of malt barley to Kirkwall; this was her first call for over a year. On the 15th, the British TOWER JULIE took 33 tons of flocor to Bremerhaven, and one week later the Dutch FRISIAN left for Turkey with general cargo, her destination being Istanbul rather than Samsun. The month had begun with the West German coaster EBERSTEIN arriving with silica bricks and wine from Andernach. The two arrivals on 28 May are worth noting. The Cypriot SKYSTEWART brought more boric acid from Bandirma, and the British ELSIE M arrived with 339 tons of chipboard from Rotterdam. Other cargoes were very much as usual; there just happened to be more of them. For instance, there were three consignments of crepe paper, the first from Lilla Edet on the 7th in LYS-CON (one of four movements on the early afternoon tide), and the next two on the 20th and 25th both from Lysekil by LYS BRIS.

June was not quite as interesting but it was pleasing to see, towards the end of the month, two British coasters in port in the steel trades. WIS berthed on the 23rd with 980 tons of steel billets from Brussels and three days later Everard's CITY arrived with 676 tons of steel beams from Ghent. On the 28th, a new vessel appeared on the Ijmuiden run - the Groningen-registered HUGO BRINKMAN. She was a brand new ship, and was identical to PAULINA BRINKMAN built in 1975. The two vessels each offered a deadweight tonnage of 1,585 tons; this figure was over twice that available on FRIDEL and 50% greater than that of JEMRIX. It would be possible, therefore, to maintain the quantity of steel imported but with fewer calls by fewer ships. July proved to be the busiest month yet for Chinese cargo, with six arrivals on two of which was palm kernel meal. There were three exports during the month. On 3 July, the Danish SATELITH took 32 portacabins to Dunkerque; on the 12th, FRISIAN took 652 tons of general cargo to Samsun and, on the next day, the West German HOHEWEG lifted 505 tons of bentonite clay for Sandnes. There were no exports at all in August. On the import side, there were three more Chinese cargoes. The general goods came in the East German MARLOW and ZUSSOW on the 12th and 18th repectively, while the West German PAMIR II brought palm kernels on the 15th. SATELITH was back in September, but this time to load general cargo for Samsun, whither ROELOF HOLWERDA departed at the end of the month. Imports continued to be dominated by steel. During the month, there were three cargoes from Ijmuiden, the ships involved being FRIDEL, KENRIX and JEMRIX, two from Brussels and Brake, and one each from Duisberg and Antwerp.

By October COASTER CONNY had become a regular caller with PVC. October's first arrival, though, was on the 7th when the Danish MERC POLARIS arrived with 1,096 tons of chipboard from Marin. It was very much the month of Danish coasters, for on the 15th OPNOR arrived with 526 tons of magnesium chloride flake from Bremen. A further Dane, SIRI MARIA, berthed on 23rd October - and this time managed to avoid contact with the West Pier - to load 299 tons of steel piling for Rotterdam. On the 26th, SATELITH was back yet again, this time loading portacabins for Boulogne. November's only export was 518 tons of bentonite clay to Sandnes, on the 10th, taken by the Danish LISE CLIPPER; she had arrived six days earlier with Chinese general cargo from Hamburg. The same owner's MARIA CLIPPER brought a similar cargo on 22 November. A large consignment of steel from Ijmuiden, 1,561 tons, was brought on 4 November by LONDONER. It was her first call, and did not take too much effort to guess her port of registry! The shipment of portacabins to Dunkerque on 6 December was taken not by SATELITH but by her sistership DANALITH. Talking of sisterships, and even more appropriately, three days earlier it was COASTER ANNY rather than COASTER CONNY which had brought PVC from Heroya. A Netherlands Antilles vessel was seen in port on December when ARBON arrived with 631 tons of PVC from Cagliari. She was one of the biggest ships to have berthed in Whitby, being 77.65 metres (252 feet) in length, and surpassed only by MERCANDIAN EXPORTER which was one metre longer. ARBON had had to wait off the harbour entrance for two days until the weather was good enough for her to be brought into port. Berthed over the festive season was the Guernsey-registered EDDYSTONE, discharging general cargo. It was unusual to see a British ship in this trade.

Above:
Outward bound for Ipswich on 7 August 1985 is the West German coaster ESTE. She had brought the penultimate cargo of transshipped Chinese general cargo from Hamburg.

Below:
The pilot cutter lies alongside Crescent Shipping's ELOQUENCE which is discharging corn gluten from Rotterdam at Endeavour Wharf on 30 December 1983.

CHAPTER 5 1980 ONWARDS:
FIGHTING THE RECESSION

The new decade opened with a new ship on the Ijmuiden run. She was the recently-built ALLIANCE, and was virtually identical to PAULINA BRINKMAN and HUGO BRINKMAN. She would make five visits to Whitby during the year. The arrival in Hamburg of the Japanese freighter HOWA MARU with cargo from China generated three shipments of trans-shipped goods across the North Sea to Whitby. The West German ESTEBURG brought 550 tons of palm kernel meal, while general cargo was on board her compatriot JAN MEEDER and the East German SEMLOW. Apart from noting that on 24 February COASTER ANNY arrived from Skien with 71m³of timber in addition to 609 tons of PVC, most of the interest in February and March was centered on exports. The Norwegian STENFOSS took bentonite clay to Sandnes on 8 February, and DANALITH departed for Port Said on the 14th with 285 tons of general cargo. Her sistership FINLITH sailed to the Algerian port on Bejaia with pipes and portacabins on 4 March and it was yet another Danish coaster, GROLLEN, which departed on 22 March with bentonite clay for Lerwick.

April's total of 25 ships was more than double that for March. Unusual among the exports were two shipments of potash. On 16 April, the Irish MALONE took 792 tons to Londonderry and on the 25th the British ANGUS took 407 tons along the east coast to Fosdyke. These were the first exports of potash from the Boulby Mine, north of Whitby, to be handled by the port, most of the mine's exports being taken to a purpose-built terminal on the Tees. However, smaller and infrequent cargoes of a specialised granular product were exported via Whitby. A major cause of the big increase in the number of ships using the port during April was the ending of the steel strike. The strike had first hit Whitby in early January when JEMRIX arrived with 750 tons of steel billets from Ijmuiden. Iron and Steel Trades Confederation pickets were at the dock gates to prevent the steel from leaving. In fact, the dockers discharged the steel into storage until the end of the strike. With the strike now ended, there was a considerable increase in the tonnage of steel passing over the wharves during April and May. April held other interest, too. The smart West German JAN GRAEBE arrived on the 13th with 1,349 tons of chipboard from Helsinki, and, on the 21st, there was a new arrival in the refractories trade when the Danish MONSUNEN arrived from Uddevalla. She brought five of the six

Much of the cargo taken to Turkey and the Middle East in the late 1970s was handled by the blue-hulled ships owned by the Dutch Holwerda company. Here, this company's FRISIAN is seen loading at Endeavour Wharf on 18 May 1979.

The former Royal Navy minesweeper HMS WISTON arrived at Whitby to be demolished on 2 November 1982. By the end of December when this photograph was taken, demolition was well under way.

shipments during the year. ANGUS took a further cargo of potash along the east coast on 1 May, this time to Great Yarmouth, and the following day FINLITH sailed to Boulogne with portacabins. The fact that trade continued at a high level in May was due to the large amount of steel being handled. Two British coasters, ECCTONIA and WIS, took steel to Antwerp, while two West Germans, STEM and GORCH FOCK, took cargoes to Hamburg. By contrast, three Hamburg-registered ships, TAFELBERG, TORSTEN and EDITH SABBAN, brought in steel coils from Bremen. Also, the Duisburg-registered RUHR brought 818 tons of steel billets from Cologne on 19 May, and returned on the 3 June to load steel for Bilbao. Reference above to the coaster STEM recalls an earlier important occasion in the recent history of Whitby port for she was, until 1976, called MARTHA FRIESECKE and as such she had brought the first consignment of steel from Ijmuiden on 9 August 1970.

Trade during the latter months of the year slipped back. Indeed, there were only thirteen vessels each month between July and December, except September (twelve) and November (sixteen). There was a brief flurry of interest in late summer. The same tide on 30 August brought the Hamburg-registered KIEKEBERG with a large cargo of 1,483 tons of steel from Moerdijk and the Plymouth-registered ROVER T with 329 tons of soya beans from Rotterdam. This was a new commodity for the port, as was the 534 tons of peat moss brought on the 3 September from Ventspils by TARTU. She was the first Russian vessel to visit the port for several years.

The traditional-style coasters owned by H. R. Mitchell were a familiar sight in many ports along the east coast of Britain, and were particularly common handling explosives in the south east. They were never regular callers at Whitby, though, so it was particularly pleasing to see ISABEL MITCHELL on 20 October and JOHN MITCHELL on 8 November. Each had brought soya beans from Rotterdam. There were seven shipments of Chinese general cargo during October and November. Mid-December saw port activity increase very briefly. On the 16th, ROSELLE berthed with 258 tons of kraft paper from Trondheim and the Panamanian VIOS brought soya bean pellets from Rotterdam. On the next day, JUPITER brought 499 tons of rape seed meal from Hamburg, her home port. In Whitby over the Christmas period was another Panamanian coaster, ELIAS JR., with a further cargo of soya bean pellets.

The 1980's had begun with three chief trades. Steel from Ijmuiden still accounted for most ship arrivals - 54 in 1980, with KENRIX bringing 19 and JEMRIX bringing 14. Next was general cargo from

Norway. TEANO handled 18 and ROSELLE 12 of the 34 sailings. The 22 consignments of Chinese general cargo had been handled by a wide variety of ships. As already stated, there were only six shipments of refractory materials. These disappeared completely from the 1981 trading figures, as did crepe paper.

The first months of 1981 indicated that Whitby was to grow in importance in the handling of cereals. Another Mitchell ship, VIOLET MITCHELL, brought soya bean pellets from Rotterdam on 19 January, while the Dover-registered HELENA JAYNE brought a further shipment on the 28th. On the same tide, the Panamanian OUDE MAAS brought soya bean meal from Zwijndrecht. Three days later, 505 tons of rice bran came from Rotterdam on the Newport-registered COLSTON. This coaster had an interesting history, having been built in 1955 by Charles Hill at Bristol for the Bristol Channel coal trade. A regular visitor to the port for many years, usually loading barley for Kirkwall, had been the Aberdeen-registered HELMSDALE. She met a sad fate in November 1980 when she grounded near Montrose as she departed for Kirkwall. She was subsequently demolished at Inverkeithing. Early in 1981, her owner chartered SAINT RONAN to take over the work. This 1966-built coaster was owned by the well-known Glasgow firm of shipowners and quarrymasters, J. and A. Gardner, whose fleet of coasters was much more familiar on the west coast of Britain than the east. When SAINT RONAN loaded malting barley for Kirkwall at Whitby in early February, it was the first visit to the port by a Gardner ship. It was not long before she was bought from Gardner's and renamed HELMSDALE to maintain that name. Oddly enough, mid-February saw two inwards shipments of malting barley from La Pallice. The Dutch HARMA brought the first on the 14th, followed nine days later by ALLIANCE, already familiar on the Ijmuiden steel run.

March was a very quiet month with only eleven arrivals, but several points of interest, Steel exports resumed after a lull. On 20 March, the West German VERENA took a shipment to Bilbao and the Dutch ST. MICHAEL took her cargo to Rotterdam. On the 4th BOGINKA became the first Polish ship to bring Chinese general cargo from Hamburg. Two days later, the Russian ENGURE arrived with peat moss from Ventspils. This cargo, used in horticulture, was for onward distribution to north west and southern England. Another large consignment of malting barley, 1,450 tons, arrived from La Pallice on the Panamanian SEA AVON on 22 March. April saw a further two Polish ships bring Chinese general cargo, NER on the 2nd and CHOCHLIK on the 9th. On 4 April, the West German OSTEDIEK arrived with 985 tons of steel plates from Taranto.

May witnessed a brief upsurge in trade. There were three exports of steel to Rotterdam and one to Antwerp, the latter taken by JOHN MITCHELL on 28 May; she had arrived four days earlier with 391 tons of corn gluten pellets. On 5 May, the Swedish NORDLANDIA had brought 1,152 tons of malt from Helsinki. Surprisingly few Swedish coasters have visited Whitby. Two days later, GAUYA was the next Russian vessel to bring peat moss from Ventspils. The interesting features of June's trade were at the end of the month. On the 26th, the Hull-registered HOOFINCH berthed with 354 tons of clay from Rotterdam and three days later the Cypriot BULK WAVE arrived with 449 tons of soya bean pellets from Rotterdam. On the next day, SATELITH was back in port discharging 999 tons of steel from Taranto. She then loaded 1,181 tons of steel destined for Bilbao. Of the thirteen arrivals in July, five were Chinese general cargo. Amongst other callers, the small West German HUBERT, registered in Friedrichstadt, arrived on 6 July with 411 tons of steel from Vejle and left for Antwerp two days later with 444 tons of steel rails.

Shipping enthusiasts who visited Whitby during August were fortunate if they saw a ship in port, for arrivals reached a new low of seven in the month. Despite this, there were two new cargoes, and 21 August was the day to see them. The Polish SWIETLIK sailed with 327 tons of waste paper to Hommelvik, and the British TOWER JULIE arrived with 763 tons of feed wheat from Littlehampton. Further waste paper was taken to Hommelvik on 17 September by the West German ULSNIS. A week later, the small Norwegian coaster IRENE took 117 tons of steel to Stavanger, and she was back in port on 10 October to discharge aluminium from Farsund. Trade continued at a low ebb in November and December. Another small Norwegian vessel, TEVLA, brought Chinese general cargo on 27 November and loaded waste paper. Three British ships visited the port in December. BARNSTAPLE TRADER brought corn gluten feed pellets while WILKS and ECCTONIA took steel to Antwerp and Rotterdam respectively.

1982 began with nine consignments of Chinese general cargo in the first two months and there were six steel export shipments during February. March had only nine ship arrivals, three of which were for steel exports. ELISABETH HOLWERDA came back to Whitby, sailing with steel for Bilbao on the 13th. HARRY MITCHELL left for Antwerp on the 16th and sailing for Stavanger on the 18th was the Norwegian BAKKETUN. The following day saw the month's only other export, 721 tons of bentonite to Sandnes on the Norwegian LEONARD. By contrast, Wharton's BRENDONIA had brought 733 tons of hectorite clay from Rotterdam on the 18th.

April, with eighteen arrivals, was the busiest month of the year. The Ijmuiden steel run, not mentioned for some time, was usually taken by HUGO BRINKMAN or PAULINA BRINKMAN, although the Dutch EXPANSA II put in a call on the 16th. The years covered so far in this survey have seen a steady move by shipowners away from the flags of traditional maritime countries such as Britain, the Netherlands and, to a lesser extent, West Germany, and instead to a more common use of "convenience flags" such as Panama and Cyprus. Now another distant nation was starting to emerge as "operator" of tonnage in European coastal trades, namely Honduras. The afternoon of 22 April saw two movements of Honduran vessels in the port. NIALED TRADER departed in ballast for Amsterdam having discharged steel pipes from Lerwick; KIMBLE arrived with a similar cargo. The stay in port of the latter ship turned out to be somewhat longer than anticipated. During her voyage from Lerwick, she got into difficulties off north-east Scotland and had to be taken in tow to Aberdeen by United Towing's YORKSHIREMAN. The owners of KIMBLE failed to lodge a guarantee of payment at Lloyds because of a dispute as to whether it should be the owners themselves or their insurance company who should make the guarantee. The immediate outcome was that United Towing asked for the ship to be arrested, and the Admiralty Marshal duly nailed a writ to the ship's mast after she had completed discharge at Endeavor Wharf. To enable other ships to be handled, KIMBLE was then moved to Eskside Wharf where she would be less of a hindrance. Fortunately for all concerned, the matter was resolved within a matter of days and KIMBLE was released, having had the distinction of being the first ship to be arrested in Whitby. A further arrival from Lerwick on 16 May was the British PEKARI; her cargo was 216 tons of scrap anchor chain. The immaculate Dutch coaster ALK berthed on the morning tide of 27 May to discharge 499 tons of silicon manganese from Rotterdam. The same tide witnessed the departure of the Cypriot BULK SEA with 504 tons of brewing malt for Antwerp. At this time, ROSELLE continued to be a regular caller, at approximately monthly intervals usually bringing in packaged timber from Norway and taking back general cargo. TEANO maintained a much more frequent link with Norway.

Unusual among the thirteen ships visiting Whitby in June was Everard's FORMALITY; she arrived on the 30th to load 342 tons of steel for Antwerp. On 4 July, HUGO BRINKMAN arrived on her eighth call of the year from Ijmuiden, and it was her final one. A new ship appeared on the route - the British SHAMROCK ENDEAVOUR. On her first call on 20 July, she brought 1,587 tons of steel. The British KAVA SOUND, skippered by her owner, W. G. Dennison, took 266 tons of construction materials to the Shetland port of Scalloway on 28 July. August was reasonably busy, with plenty to interest ship-spotting holidaymakers, unlike the previous year. On the morning tide of the 7th, the West German ADOLPH FLINT arrived with 720 tons of anchor chains from Sullom Voe. Also arriving was another, but more modern West German vessel, WARFLETH, with 1,015 tons of chipboard from Karlsruhe, far inland on the Rhine some 636 kilometres (398 miles) up river from Rotterdam. The import of chipboard from Karlsruhe (or Duisburg or Rotterdam) has been a continuing feature of trade through Whitby harbour in subsequent years. The final day of August saw the departure of the East German NIENHAGEN with 633 tons of steel for Turku. It was common to see East German coasters bringing in Chinese general cargo, but far less common to see one taking an outward cargo.

There was little of interest in September, although another consignment of timber from Karlsruhe arrived in mid-month. The ship involved was UTE V, another West German vessel of a type being seen increasingly often in our ports. Such coasters have a very low profile, sometimes with collapsible wheelhouse and masts, to permit passage far inland on European rivers and canals. The first day of October brought NORTH SOUND from Scapa Flow with a cargo of construction materials. The morning tide three days later heralded the arrival of the Danish HERMANN C. BOYE with 948 tons of PVC from the Libyan port of Zuara, and FRIDEL with steel from Ijmuiden. On this occasion, she loaded a return cargo of 69 tons of steel billets. Close observers of the Whitby shipping scene were now becoming accustomed to the latest coaster designs, especially the modern low air-draught vessels mentioned above. It came as something of a shock, therefore, to find a traditional, bridge-amidships coaster in port at the end of the month. Flying the flag of Panama, she was called SALOME and arrived on 28 October with 709 tons of soya beans from Hamburg. Unusually for a ship under the Panamanian flag, she was not registered in Panama itself but in the port of Colon. Her outline was very familiar and a little research soon made it clear why. She was built by Clelands at Wallsend in 1955 as CONTINUITY for Everard's, a name which she bore until 1977. It was indeed a pleasant surprise to find her still trading around our shores. Perhaps it was to be expected that the final two months of the year could not produce anything to equal the visit of SALOME. Indeed there were only eighteen arrivals during those two months. The year ended, then, with chipboard accounting for one cargo per month, soya beans for two, and Chinese general for one or two. Other arrivals included the usual steel, mainly imports, Norwegian general and, occasionally, PVC.

At times, this narrative has departed briefly from its account of mercantile trade to look at other events of interest in the port area. We cannot leave 1982 without noting the arrival of a warship for demolition on 2 November. She was HMS WISTON, a former Royal Navy minesweeper, which had been bought by the Sheffield-based firm of Kitson Vickers and which was moored in the upper harbour for demolition purposes. It was thought that other warships may be brought to Whitby to meet their fate, but to date, WISTON has been the only arrival.

The main shipbrokers and agents in Whitby had been Thos. E. Kettlewell and Son, a Goole-based firm. At the beginning of 1982, Kettlewells handed over their Whitby operation to a new company, and henceforth the brokerage and agency work was handled by the firm which traded as Whitby Port Services. Although 1982 had witnessed an increased tonnage of 10,000 tonnes in cargo handled over the total for 1981, there were indications that the future was starting to look bleak for commercial operations in the port. The Whitby Gazette on 14 January 1983 proclaimed in a bold headline "Docks Jobs Shock", and reported the prospect of redundancies among the dockers or even cuts in wages. January, traditionally a poor month for trade anyway, seemed to bear out the gloomy forecasts for only six ships were handled during the month. February's total did improve to eleven, but it was still a dismal figure. On the 5th, the London-registered ELLEN W brought a Chinese general cargo from Hamburg - a rare British ship on this run. Four days later, NORTH SOUND returned to load 151 tons of plasterboard for Kirkwall. The four consignments of steel from Ijmuiden were shared by PAULINA BRINKMAN and SHAMROCK ENDEAVOUR.

The trading figures reveal that there were no imports or exports of Norwegian general cargo at this time. This was not as worrying as it may appear at first because the service was, in fact, being reorganised quite radically by its operator, Stream Line, and Whitby was henceforth to be the British terminal, without further calls to Goole. Consequently, March saw an increase in ship arrivals to eighteen. Of these, THURSO accounted for three and TEANO for two. These two vessels have continued to visit Whitby for the next five years and have established a highly successful service between Norway and Whitby. The only other item of interest in March was the continued arrival of chipboard. The West German EDINA brought 821 tons from Rotterdam on the 22nd and was followed the next day by her compatriot LAGUNE with 186 tons from Karlsruhe. She had discharged the balance of her cargo at Selby. She, too, has become a regular caller in the last five years. Indeed, it must be admitted that this period has suffered from a degree of monotony in terms of ships. This is not to say that trade has been slack. In 1984, over 184,000 tonnes of cargo were handled, this total coming second only to the 191,000 tonnes of 1974. It is significant that the latter was conveyed in 282 ships with only a handful of return cargoes. In 1984, though, there were 245 ships handled, many of these conveying both inward and outward cargoes. This applies particularly in the Norwegian trade.

It consequently becomes more difficult to find items of interest as we return to our chronological account. In May 1983, the most noteworthy feature was the visit of two London and Rochester Co. ships. TARQUENCE arrived from Ijmuiden on the 11th, this being her second call of the year on this route, while CADENCE berthed on the 20th to load 522 tons of steel for Antwerp. There were two shipments of plywood from Rotterdam, both in Danish coasters. Our old friend SATELITH arrived on the 4th, and JENCLIPPER on the 12th. Two days later, another Danish vessel arrived. Called GROLLEN, she brought 486 tons of PVC from Zuara. There was a new ship on the Ijmuiden route on 4 June when SHAMROCK ENTERPRISE, a sistership of SHAMROCK ENDEAVOUR, brought 1,593 tons of steel. UTE V and WARFLETH brought the month's two consignments of chipboard. The oddity of the month, though, was the visit to Whitby of two different ships bearing the same name. On the 7th, SABINE, registered at San Lorenzo in Honduras, sailed with 518 tons of steel to Antwerp, and on the 30th the West German SABINE took 991 tons of steel to Hamburg.

Just when it seemed that chipboard was well-established, it is surprising to find that none was handled in July or August. Despite that, July was a busy month with 21 callers. A couple of Dutch vessels provided some variety at the end of the month. Beck's

On 31 July 1983, Beck's VINCENT is discharging soya bean pallets from Rotterdam at Endeavour Wharf.

Holidaymakers would be lining the harbour side on the morning of 4 August 1983 to watch THURSO arrive at the end of her regular voyage from Norway.

VINCENT berthed on the 28th with 609 tons of corn gluten pellets from Rotterdam, while the splendidly maintained JOHN V arrived two days later to load 505 tons of lager malt for Bremen. The only unusual feature of August's trade was the departure on the 27th of the small British coaster LABRICA with 351 tons of scrap steel for Mulheim. A further consignment of lager malt for Bremen was taken by FASTNET, a Panamanian flag coaster, on 20 September, and the British SILLOTH STAG departed for Vejle and Hamburg on the 23rd with 894 tons of steel coils.

Sunday, 2 October, was noteworthy in that there were two London and Rochester Co. ships in port. INSISTENCE was discharging corn gluten pellets from Rotterdam, and XANTHENCE was discharging soya beans, also from Rotterdam. INSISTENCE sailed on the p.m. tide of the 3rd, and TARQUENCE arrived from Ijmuiden on the next tide. A big cargo of 1,085 tons of steel coils was shipped to La Spezia by the Panamanian ELLIE on 12 November. In February 1981, this coaster had been attacked off the Irish coast by supporters of the I.R.A. and she sank after explosive charges had been detonated. At the time, she was called NELLIE M and was on a voyage from Blyth to Coleraine. However, she was salvaged, sold and returned to commercial service. Chipboard arrived at Whitby from Moerdijk on the Cypriot LADY ANITA on 20 November. A further consignment arrived at the end of the month on the British HOOPRIDE. The much newer HOOCREEK arrived on 21 December to load 1,084 tons of steel coils for Antwerp.

Although the first four months of 1984 brought little that was novel to the port, this should not hide the fact that trade through the port was now much healthier than had been the case twelve months earlier. A couple of arrivals in late January possibly justify a mention. On the 25th, the Danish ARKTIS STAR arrived with 1,059 tons of PVC from Zuara and, three days later, the Norwegian NAFOSS brought 582 tons of aluminium from Sundalsora. February revealed a truly typical trading pattern. Imports were steel, soya beans, corn gluten, and general cargo from Norway and China; exports were steel coils and general cargo to Norway. The only omission was chipboard, but this arrived in March, as did one cargo of hectorite. The latter was brought by the British HOO WILLOW from Rotterdam on the 30th. Two days earlier, the Norwegian LEOPOLD brought 1,011 tons of packaged timber from Namsos. She was one of four arrivals on the early morning tide; the others were THURSO (with Norwegian general), MIROW (with Chinese general) and SHAMROCK ENDEAVOUR (with steel from

Ijmuiden).

A further cargo of aluminium arrived on 19 May. This comprised 277 tons brought by the Danish SALTA from Ardalstangen. The month also saw two old friends in new guise. On 12 May, NER berthed with Chinese general cargo. She had called previously in this trade but now she was no longer flying the Polish flag. She had been sold and was trading under the flag of Honduras, registered in San Lorenzo, but without a change of name. On the 31st, the Panamanian LATONA arrived to load 497 tons of steel for Rotterdam. She had been a familiar caller at east coast ports when she traded as PETREL for the General Steam Navigation Co. Of the five steel shipments from Ijmuiden during June, three were handled by SHAMROCK ENTERPRISE. On two occasions, she took return cargoes of tinplate and pallets. On 23 June, the West German HALSTENBEK, a vessel of classic coaster design and dating from 1960, brought 809 tons of barley from Inverness.

It is obviously coincidental, but many of the more interesting ships seemed to be arriving towards the end of each month. For instance, the Dutch ATLANTIC SEA berthed on 26 July with 756 tons of PVC from Porsgrunn, not from Zuara as had been the case in recent months. Two days later, JOHN V was back to discharge corn gluten from her home port of Rotterdam. Dating from 1957, she still made a splendid sight having been maintained in excellent condition by her owners and crew. On the 29th, LADY ANITA arrived with 1,141 tons of chipboard, again from Rotterdam. A most unusual caller on 25 August was the American oil rig supply vessel HARTEBEEST, registered in Morgan City. She arrived at 2.15 a.m. with 72 tons of rig equipment and departed at 5.15 p.m. with 208 tons of steel pipes.

September proved to be the busiest month for some time. There were no less than six arrivals with Norwegian general cargo. The first of these was NAFOSS on the 3rd, and she returned on the 16th. On the 7th, the Honduran flag ORIEND sailed for Rotterdam with 228 tons of paint, and later on the same day the Danish BEATRINES sailed for Antwerp with 594 tons of firebricks. The same tide brought another Dane, LILLE - KAREN, with 331 tons of wire rod in coil from Hamburg. The West German JANE berthed to discharge 501 tons of steel plates from Duisburg on the 11th and, four days later, the Danish LOTTE TY arrived with 1,432 tons of timber and insulation board from Szczecin. The final point of note in this busy month was the arrival from Ijmuiden of TARQUENCE on the 25th. This was her final call as a regular vessel on this route. The Whitby

Gazette on 28 September bore the headline "Trade Surge" and reported that port facilities were so stretched during the month that three ships had been turned away. Trade continued to flourish to the end of the year. A different London and Rochester ship arrived from Ijmuiden on 15 October when BOISTERENCE berthed with 766 tons of steel. She was not to become a regular on the route, though. The familiar ROSELLE made a return to the port bringing 880 tons of packaged timber from Namsos on 22 October. She returned on 13 November with a slightly larger cargo. The West German CLAUDIA L was now bringing in one cargo of chipboard per month from Karlsruhe or Rotterdam. Built in 1983, she was one of the new generation of low air draught coasters and was the first of a series to be built by Hermann Surken at Papenburg on the river Ems. On 27 November, the British RIVER DART brought 767 tons of steel from Ijmuiden, returning the following day with 272 tons of tinplate. She is one of the three ships working from Ijmuiden in this trade at the time of writing. The only variation in the usual trades in December was on the 5th when the West German AROSITA took 1,587 tons of steel coils to Hamburg.

1985 began with a return of Chinese general cargo after a 2½ month break. The vessel was the Honduran NADIR. She was an interesting vessel, having been built in 1960 as SAINT MODAN for J and A Gardner. She bore the names MODAN, NIALED, MONIQUE and MONICA prior to being renamed NADIR. Lloyd's Register of Shipping has failed to note that she was called MONICA for a period. The East German RAKOW brought a second consignment of Chinese general cargo on 18 January. Imports of steel from Ijmuiden were now being shared by SHAMROCK ENDEAVOUR, SHAMROCK ENTERPRISE and RIVER DART. An exception occurred on 19 January when SEA AVON arrived with a very large cargo of 1,845 tons. Registered in Nassau, she was the first Bahamas flag ship to call at Whitby. She was also unusual in being one of a group of four coasters built in Japan for the British company Seacon. Very rarely do European coastal shipowners go to Japan for new vessels. February and March were less interesting. A new ship appeared with general cargo from Norway; she was SUNDLAND, herself Norwegian, which arrived on 20 February and departed two days later with 416 tons of crushing balls for Kirkenes. Of note in March was the appearance of two identical former London and Rochester coasters, both with soya beans from Rotterdam. On the 9th, GORE (ex ELOQUENCE) arrived, followed on the 29th by LATEN (ex BLATENCE). Each vessel was still registered in

Rochester. It should be noted that the London and Rochester Co. was now using its "other" title of Crescent Shipping in its commercial activities.

We have to wait until the end of April to find a couple of items of interest. On the 29th, the Honduran FLARDINGHA brought a new cargo - 999 tons of granite chips from Belfast. The following day, TEANO was in port to handle her usual general cargo to and from Norway, but the eagle-eyed observer would have noted on her stern that she was no longer registered in Trondheim but in Kristiansund. In mid-May, there were two imports of PVC, the first on the Panamanian BORG and the second on the Danish LOTTELITH. A further cargo of crushing balls for Kirkenes was taken by the Norwegian JOETT on 11 May. It was something of a surprise to see the familiar PAULINA BRINKMAN arrive in port with 1,114 tons of steel on 26 May. On this occasion, though, she brought her cargo from Hamburg. June was one of the most interesting months for some time. A further load of granite chips arrived on the 8th, brought by NESTINDUR. She seems to have been the first Faroese coaster to call at Whitby. An unusual cargo of 522 tons of granulated fertiliser was shipped to Ghent on the 26th by the Panamanian DUET. The West German ATOLL brought three consignments of chipboard from Karlsruhe during the month. Mention has already been made of the change in port of registry of TEANO. In fact, she and THURSO were transferred from the ownership of J. P. Strom to that of Gunnar Kjonnoy. It was interesting to observe two of Strom's newer, larger ships in port during June. On the 1st, TELLO arrived from Rotterdam. Built in 1974 as LYSHOLMEN for Lys Line, she had just been renamed from NORNANBORG, a name which she had borne since 1980. Her sistership TINTO, built in 1975 as LYSFOSS again for Lys Line, arrived from Namsos on the a.m. tide of the 18th. Coincidentally, she was only fifteen minutes behind THURSO. She quickly discharged her cargo for she departed for Antwerp on the next tide.

July, too, saw plenty of interest in the port. On the 1st, the Norwegian SCOTT arrived with 985 tons of packaged timber from Namsos. She had also only recently been renamed, having previously traded as LEOPOLD under which name she had visited Whitby in March 1984. The Danish DORTE STAR arrived to load 697 tons of steel for Copenhagen and Vejle on the 3rd. Two days later, Whitby bade farewell to SHAMROCK ENDEAVOUR, and two weeks later welcomed a brand new ship to the Ijmuiden run, the Dutch STEEL SPRINTER which berthed on 19 July with 1,327 tons.

TEANO is seen at Endeavour Wharf on 29 October 1986. Her bow bears the letters "GK" showing that at this time she had come into the ownership of Gunnar Kjonnoy.

A mobile crane lifts chipboard from LAGUNE at Endeavour Wharf. It will be noticed that the rail tracks remain in situ although they have not been used since the late 1970s.

Other items of note during the month included the export of 580 tons of steel to Viana de Castelo by the West German HENDRIK on the 12th, and a fortnight later the departure of another West German, VAGABUND, with 800 tons of steel scrap for Stralsund. August produced nothing of note, but September did have some interest. On the 10th, THURSO arrived with her port of registry changed to Kristiansund. One week later, the Danish ELLEN LYO arrived with the final Chinese general cargo, only 194 tons of it. The trade with China was increasingly being handled by large, purpose-built container ships serving Tilbury and the quantity of break-bulk cargo being trans-shipped was now decreasing rapidly. The smart Norwegian coaster GARDEN took 415 tons of crushing balls to Trondheim on 19 September, and the following day witnessed the final arrival of SHAMROCK ENTERPRISE.

We had to wait for over a month to see her replacement, for it was on 24 October that the new STEEL SHUTTLE, a sistership of STEEL SPRINTER, arrived with 1,622 tons of steel from Ijmuiden. She sailed the next day with 136 tons of tinplate. 26 October was a busy day for the port. On the a.m. tide, the West German GRAUERORT, registered in Ostrauderfehn, arrived with 548 tons of soya beans from Rotterdam. Also, the Danish LILLE-TOVE arrived to load 336 tons of potash for Bergen. A further Dane, PEDER MOST, arrived on the p.m. tide with 1,026 tons of PVC from Zuara. It cannot go unmentioned that the port handled six cargoes of chipboard during the month, five of them brought by LAGUNE and the sixth by her sistership ATOLL which sailed on the 17th with 334 tons of steel pipes for Neuss. The arrival of PAULINA BRINKMAN in May with steel from Hamburg has already been noted; she was back in Whitby on 13 November with 1,442 tons of steel - from Ijmuiden. This was very much a one-off cargo, as was the 1,600 tons brought five days later by the West German EDITH SABBAN. A most unusual import on 25 November was 517 tons of feed barley from Cowes, brought by the Dutch TWEBRO.

By December, it was clear that LAGUNE was becoming the usual vessel to bring in chipboard. She made three calls during this month, making one of her visits doubly profitable by taking a back cargo of 397 tons of cast iron scrap to Duisburg. On the 13th, LILLE-TOVE returned to load 445 tons of potash for Bergen. Six days later, NAFOSS berthed with 701 tons of aluminium from Sundalsora.

To all intents and purposes, our story is now complete. 1986 began, and continued, with three main trades providing the basis for Whitby port's prosperity. Firstly, there was the general cargo trade to and from Norway, handled almost exclusively by TEANO and THURSO. Secondly came the import of steel from Ijmuiden. This was handled by thee ships - the British RIVER DART and the Dutch STEEL SPRINTER and STEEL SHUTTLE. Other vessels do put in occasional appearances; it was pleasing to welcome back HUGO BRINKMAN on 7 February 1986. The third trade is the import of chipboard from the river Rhine, usually Karlsruhe, and mostly brought by LAGUNE or ATOLL. There are still occasional cargoes of PVC from Zuara, imports of soya beans and fertilisers, and exports of steel. During the last three decades, Whitby port has seen many different cargoes pass over its wharves and hundreds of different ships tie up alongside. The future in international trade and shipping is always difficult to predict; all that can be said is that with its efficient and hard-working labour force and forward-looking management it will continue to offer an excellent service to its customers and prove that it will remain a modern seaport.

Index of ships listed in the text.

The West German coaster LAGUNE is seen here at Endeavour Wharf discharging a cargo of chipboard on 29 October 1986.